UNTO THE LEAST OF THESE

UNTO THE LEAST OF THESE

SPECIAL EDUCATION IN THE CHURCH

Andrew H. Wood
with E. Ellen Glanville
and LaVerne A. Weber

REGULAR BAPTIST PRESS
1300 North Meacham Road
Post Office Box 95500
Schaumburg, Illinois 60195

Library of Congress Cataloging in Publication Data

Wood, Andrew H., 1927—
  Unto the least of these.

  1. Church work with the mentally handicapped. I. Glanville, E. Ellen,
1934— . II. Weber, LaVerne A., 1936— . III. Title.
BV4461.W66 1984 259'.4 84—16077
ISBN 0-87227-099-8

C O N T E N T S

Section Four
Principles Of Working With
The Mentally Retarded *75*

Appendices

PREFACE

The history of the fundamental local church in America indicates a definite lack of programming for the handicapped, particularly the mentally retarded. Yet, these precious ones, set aside through no fault of their own, present a real challenge to local churches seeking to reach their communities for Jesus Christ.

Shepherds, Inc., The Regular Baptist Agency for the Mentally Retarded, was raised up of God in 1957 to meet this challenge. During the years since then, Shepherds has seen a steadily growing network of special Sunday School classes and special church ministries spring up. A Christ-centered residential program has also come into being—The SHEPHERDS HOME AND SCHOOL, Union Grove, Wisconsin, where the mentally retarded of all ages live in a splendid Christian environment.

It is the earnest prayer of Shepherds that many mentally retarded persons may come to know Him Who said:

> . . .*Suffer little children, and forbid them not, to come unto me:*
> *for of such is the kingdom of heaven (Matt. 19:14).*

INTRODUCTION

Bear ye one another's burdens,
and so fulfil the law of Christ (Gal 6:2).

T he mentally retarded and their families represent a vast mission field
scarcely touched for Jesus Christ. Many of these families are looking
for help and hope, yet all too frequently they find little more than scorn or
indifference. As more and more programs are developed on the community
level to meet the physical, emotional, educational and social needs of the
mentally retarded, fundamental Bible-believing churches should make provision for the most important need of all—the spiritual. Thus, it is not only
the *responsibility* of local churches to reach this segment of the population
for Jesus Christ, but it is their glorious *privilege* to show them the way.

This manual offers detailed instruction for Christians burdened to minister to the mentally retarded through the local church. The material presented has been shared in hundreds of special education workshops, taught
in Shepherds College of Special Education, and successfully put into practice
in local churches throughout America.

It is the prayer of the authors that God will use this volume to stir the
hearts of many Christians to become involved in reaching America's 6.7
million mentally retarded and their families for Jesus Christ.

Section One

MENTAL RETARDATION— WHAT IS IT ALL ABOUT?

In spite of widespread promotion of the public media and government agencies, few people clearly understand the concept of mental retardation. Many misconceptions and misunderstandings still exist, such as the common one that mental retardation is the same as mental illness. Such a misconception shows that mental retardation is perhaps more a subject of conversation than of clear definition and understanding.

This section is designed to clear up some of the common misconceptions and misunderstandings, to develop an adequate understanding of the nature and characteristics of mental retardation, and to consider causes and problems . . . all with a view of ministering effectively to the mentally retarded within the local church.

Give me now wisdom and knowledge, that I may go out
and come in before this people . . . (2 Chron. 1:10).

1

WHO ARE THE
MENTALLY RETARDED?

Definition

The common definition for mental retardation as given by the American Association of Mental Deficiency (AAMD—1983) is:

"Mental retardation refers to significantly subaverage general intellectual functioning existing concurrently with deficits in adaptive behavior and manifested during the developmental period."

Mental retardation is usually recognized by slowness in achieving developmental skills such as sitting, walking, talking, dressing, feeding and toileting; a limited ability to learn and put learning to use; immature social awareness, behavior and judgment; and limited vocational and independent living skills.

Subaverage general intellectual functioning generally refers to an individual's ability to learn in academic or practical areas, to reason or solve problems, to memorize or remember information, and to understand or comprehend. It is measured by reference to Intelligence Quotient (IQ) scores. (Scores below seventy fall into the retarded range.)

Adaptive behavior refers to the personal, independent living, social or functional skills that allow a person to cope with the social and cultural demands of his environment. Included are such skills as caring for one's personal needs while living independently in society, social graces and attitudes, proper conduct or behavior, proper respect for other individuals and property, and the ability to earn a living.

The *developmental period* refers to the period from birth to age twenty-one.

Mental retardation is a *condition,* not a physical or mental illness. Deficits or impairments, as noted, are characteristics of the condition. It is possible for a person to be considered mentally retarded at one age and not at another. For example, a mildly retarded individual may have difficulty during school years but, because he has learned vocational and independent living skills, he is able to live successfully in the community as an adult; thus, he is not considered to be mentally retarded. Many mildly retarded children are not identified or considered to be retarded until they begin to have difficulties in school.

It is also possible for a person to function on a mentally retarded level because of other handicapping conditions such as autism, emotional disturbance and deprived environment.

General Facts

An overview of some prevalent established facts in the field of mental retardation includes:

1. Mental Retardation conveys the concept that a person has a limited ability to learn and do academic work. It is a condition or state, not an illness or disease.
2. Using the commonly accepted figure of three percent of the population for estimating the number of mentally retarded persons, there are more than 6.7 million Americans so classified. **Thus, a mentally retarded child is born every five minutes** (Cornwall, 1969). This is a large segment of our population.
3. The mentally retarded affect the lives of millions of other individuals in their families and communities.
4. Mental retardation is more common than any of the following: blindness, cerebral palsy, muscular dystrophy, diabetes (Hahn & Raasch, 1969).
5. The identification of children as mentally retarded increases significantly during the early school years.
6. Observation and educational research concludes that there are various levels or degress of mental retardation.
7. Most retarded individuals live with families or in group homes within the community. The approximately two to four percent who are served in institutions are usually more severely retarded. Therefore, the retarded and their families are found in most levels of society.
8. Most families with a retarded child do not attend church regularly (Hawley, 1979).

9. The mentally retarded are people who have the same basic needs as all other people (love, acceptance, understanding, success).

Classification

All mentally retarded individuals are not affected to the same extent or degree. Classification is normally made according to the severity of impairment, the level of intellectual functioning or intelligence, and some reference to adaptive behavior or the ability of the individual to function independently in his society or culture. Because these factors are often interrelated, there are no ironclad classification systems. However, the following classifications and attendant characteristics are the most common ones referred to in professional and educational circles:

1. *Mildly Retarded Individuals*
   a. Have an approximate IQ score of 55–69
   b. Often referred to as Educable Mentally Retarded (EMR)
   c. May achieve academic skills through the 5th or 6th grade
   d. Can learn satisfactory social skills and behaviors
   e. Usually identified in a school setting
   f. May function independently/semi-independently in employment or community settings
   g. Comprise approximately 89 percent of all mentally retarded persons
2. *Moderately Retarded Individuals*
   a. Have approximate IQ scores of 40–54
   b. Often referred to as Trainable Mentally Retarded (TMR)
   c. May achieve limited functional academic skills of kindergarten through 3rd grade
   d. May develop basic self-help skills
   e. Benefit from training in social and vocational skills
   f. Can learn to perform simple vocational and job skills
   g. Usually live and work in sheltered or supervised environments
   h. Comprise approximately six percent of all mentally retarded persons
3. *Severely Retarded Individuals*
   a. Have approximate IQ of 25–39
   b. Develop some limited speech and communication skills
   c. May learn to care for their basic personal needs
   d. May have some physical handicaps
   e. Are capable of some limited vocational skills in closely supervised training centers
   f. Comprise approximately 3.5 percent of all mentally retarded persons

4. *Profoundly Retarded Individuals*
   a. Have approximate IQ scores of below 25
   b. Have definite speech, motor and coordination problems
   c. Often have multiple physical handicaps
   d. May learn some basic self-care skills
   e. Have severe physical handicaps, and have minimal capacity to function in the sensorimotor areas (integration of information received from senses of vision, hearing and touch with the movement of the eyes, arms and hands, feet and legs)
   f. Will always require total care, often in institutional settings
   g. Comprise approximately 1.5 percent of all mentally retarded persons

Causes

Professionals from many disciplines carry on a complex search for the causes of mental retardation. Underlying the search for causation is the hope of a cure and the anticipation of prevention. Although 250 known medical or biological causes have been identified, these causes account for less than twenty percent of the cases of mental retardation. Most causes that have been identified are associated with the severe levels of retardation. The following is a summary of the main causes of mental retardation:

A. *Infection or disease* during pregnancy or after birth. German measles (rubella) and RH blood factor incompatibility can cause a baby to be born retarded. Meningitis and encephalitis are the most common diseases that may affect the mental development of a young child.
B. *Toxic agents* taken by the mother during pregnancy or by the child after birth may cause retardation. When the expectant mother takes certain prescription medications or drugs like LSD, or drinks alcohol, the baby may be born retarded. If a small child ingests lead paint chips or uses ceramic dishes or objects that have been improperly fired, he can develop lead poisoning which can result in mental retardation.
C. *Brain damage* may be the result of trauma or a physical agent. Specific examples in this grouping are trauma or injury during the birth process, premature birth, oxygen deprivation or injury due to accident or child abuse.
D. *Metabolic and nutritional factors*
   These factors comprise the largest number of specific causes of retardation. Some of these factors are hereditary. Specific examples are Galac-

tosemia (the inability to metabolize sugar found in milk), Phenylketonuria (the inability to change the protein phenylaline to tyrosine), the Hypothyroidism or Cretinism.

E. *Chromosomal abnormalities*

Chromosomal abnormalities causing mental retardation have been a major area of preventive research since the 1950s. Approximately seventy-five to one hundred different types have been identified. Downs Syndrome is the most well-known example of this grouping and accounts for 5-6% of all retarded persons. Downs Syndrome is more common in mothers over thirty-five. Some basic characteristics of Downs Syndrome are slanted eyes or mongoloid appearance, large protruding tongue, short stubby fingers, broad and short neck, visual problems and poor muscle tone.

F. *Unknown prenatal factors*

These include conditions that are present at birth such as cranial and cerebral malformations. Microcephalus (small cranial or brain area) and Hydrocephalus (extra large brain or cranial area) are two specific examples.

No known medical cause exists for the largest group (80%) of the mentally retarded. The mildly retarded comprising approximately 75% of this group are retarded due to multiple psychological, environmental, genetic factors or other non-medical conditions. The relationship of these factors to one another and to the field of mental retardation is not clearly known or understood. The most commonly accepted view is the assumption that there is an undeterminable interaction between genetic, physical, psychological and environmental factors. Many in this mildly retarded group would have difficulty in school but could function independently within their community settings.

2

CHARACTERISTICS OF THE MENTALLY RETARDED

In spite of the large public special education awareness program, many people do not really know what the retarded are like. All the retarded do not look or act the same. They are not dumb or dumb looking. They are not necessarily poorly behaved or mentally ill. Remember, they have the same basic human needs as normal people, namely, love, understanding, acceptance and achievement or success. They do not need pity or sympathy. The majority do not need to be taken care of for the rest of their lives. They are not beyond help or hope!

A. *General characteristics*

Although each retarded individual is unique, some general characteristics may be defined for the group. Among these are:

    1. Developmental Delays

        These are evident in achieving basic developmental skills such as turning over, sitting, crawling, grasping, walking, feeding, talking, dressing, toileting and speech/language.

    2. Sub-average Intellectual Functioning

        Learning takes place more slowly, response time is much longer, and they are not able to compete with or keep up with their normal peers. Their rate of intellectual growth in one calendar year is approximately ½ to ¾ that of the normal child. They develop perceptual readiness (ability to understand what they see, hear and do) more slowly.

3. Attention Deficits

The retarded seem to have short attention spans, may be distractible or hyperactive, and demonstrate perseveration (continuance of any activity without stopping, such as coloring red all over a page or repeating one word). Problems may exist because they are not able to discriminate between important stimuli, or they concentrate on one area to the exclusion of all others, or they cannot organize that which is perceived.

4. Generalization Deficits

The retarded learn best by the use of concrete examples and materials. They have a limited ability to understand and use abstract concepts and ideas. There is also a marked inability to adapt or associate ideas, events, information, or skills from previously learned situations. Poor reasoning and judgment skills also are evident. Because of these factors, it is difficult for them to apply spiritual truths in changing situations.

5. Memory Deficits

These may be deficits either of short or long term memory skills although the primary area of difficulty is the short term memory. Therefore, the retarded have difficulty benefitting from past experience, projecting beyond the immediate present, learning or memorizing material, learning to play games, remembering how to go somewhere, and getting to a place on time. Thus it is necessary that teaching experiences be repeated a number of times for learning to transpire.

6. Motivation Deficit

The retarded do not demonstrate the normal tendency to learn out of curiosity, or for learning's sake, or as the result of natural exposure. Because they are self-centered, they tend not to be motivated by normal inner or external motivators. The significant person in their environment may become the chief motivational force in their lives.

7. Physical or Sensory Deficits

As a group, the retarded demonstrate more physical deficits than the same population of normal persons. Many of the retarded have multiple physical deficits.

The retarded have both fine and gross motor problems and poor coordination skills because of deficits in the functioning of their central nervous system. These deficits may be illustrated in difficulties with walking up or down stairs, buttoning, zipping, tying, cutting, running, jumping, hopping, throwing and catching.

Hearing, vision, and speech problems, colds and respiratory problems are common. A lack of muscle tone in the tongue results in drooling in adults as well as children. There may also be limitations in physical strength and endurance as well as smallness of stature. The presence of epilepsy or seizure activity and cerebral palsy may also be evident.

8. Social/Emotional Problems

These problems are characterized by poor self-images, expectancy of failure, inability to get along with one another, resistance to change from the established routine, self-abusive behaviors, immature social skills and sudden outbursts of anger, frustration and fear.

B. *Spiritual characteristics*

The mentally retarded have the same basic spiritual needs as all other individuals. Because of sin, they need the message of the gospel. They are aware of or can be taught the difference between right and wrong. They can learn spiritual truths when taught on a concrete level and within their mental functioning range. Since the majority are mildly and moderately retarded, they can and will respond to the gospel if believers present a clear and simple message using much repetition of the truths. **The second coming of Christ (rapture of the Church) is a very important spiritual truth to the believing retarded.**

C. *Specific group characteristics*

These are related directly to the degree of retardation and physical handicaps. Therefore, there is a direct correlation to the classification system.

1. **mildly retarded**—Educable (EMR—IQ 55-69)

This is the largest classification group, comprising 89% of the retarded. They often cannot be distinguished by outward physical appearance. (There is considerable variation on the academic level within this range. They may achieve anywhere from a second to a sixth grade level in reasoning, academics, vocational and social skills by their late teen years.) Basic communication skills are intact. They are capable of developing adequate social skills. They may achieve vocational skills to function in unskilled and semi-skilled job areas. After their school years, they may live and work independently in the community and some may not be considered retarded.

2. **moderately retarded**—Trainable (TMR—IQ 40-54)

As a group, the moderately retarded may demonstrate more physical handicaps than the mildly retarded. There is a tendency toward overweight, poor posture, respiratory, visual, and auditory problems. There are a variety of perceptual motor problems (integrating that which is seen, heard, or felt with movement of arms, hands, legs, feet, etc.) such as eye/hand coordination, balance, spatial relationships, and deficits in processing words and sounds that they hear. Some communication and language problems also exist in approximately ninety percent of this group. More severe academic problems also exist with an expected achievement level of kindergarten to second grade by their late teens. The emphasis is on functional academic areas, self-care, social adjustments and communication skills. Social and emotional problems are more prevalent with extremes from destructive and violent behavior to withdrawal or self-abusive behaviors. This group can learn vocational skills so they can function in sheltered workshops or closely supervised employment areas.

3. **severe-profoundly retarded**—(IQ 39 and below)

This group is characterized by the most severe mental and educational deficits, as well as the most severe crippling physical handicaps. Severe sensori-motor deficits, language handicaps and social immaturity are common. Seizure activity is also more prevalent. A variety of maladaptive behaviors have to be dealt with in working with this group. They are, for the most part, dependent upon others to care for them. Some can learn to perform simple tasks and to take care of basic self-care needs. Many are cared for in institutional settings, group homes, foster homes or nursing homes.

D. *Epilepsy*

Convulsive disorders, seizures, or "fits," referred to as epilepsy, are often found in mentally retarded persons.

Epilepsy refers to the sudden or abnormal discharge of electrical energy by the brain, resulting in a variety of symptoms: muscle contractions or convulsions, loss of consciousness, staring, daydreaming, rhythmic body movements, head dropping, chewing or smacking, incoherent speech, sudden changes in behavior, crying out, lack of response, falling, body rigidity, loss of bladder or bowel control and the experience of a warning sign called an *aura*—numbness, sounds, odors, or visual images.

Epilepsy is diagnosed by an observation of seizures, occurrences or symptoms and medical procedures such as an electroencephalogram (EEG) and a brain CAT scan. In a majority of cases, seizure activity can be controlled by various seizure medications. Epilepsy does not affect one's intelligence unless it interferes with learning, but it does affect a person's life-style because of the prejudice in society.

From a review of the professional literature, a long list of types or subtypes of seizures may be noted. The grouping of symptoms usually is the basis for classification (or typing) of seizures, consisting of three major kinds of seizures.

1. **Grand Mal seizures**—characterized by a loss of consciousness, stiffness of body, violent jerking of the body, falling, and loss of bladder

or bowel control. The seizures last one to five minutes and leave the person drowsy, disoriented, and lacking in memory of what has just occurred. This person may experience the warning signal (aura).

2. **Petit Mal seizures**—commonly called absence seizures, are characterized by non-response, staring, daydreaming, or twitching. They are of short duration (1-30 seconds) and may not be noticed by others who are near the person. The person normally resumes activity after the seizure is finished.

3. **Psycho-Motor seizures**—characterized by incoherent speech, crying out, repetitive body movements, violent actions or outbursts, confusion or disorientation. There is no loss of consciousness but the individual is confused and lacks awareness of what has occurred. Such seizures are of lesser duration than the Grand Mal but longer than Petit Mal seizures.

E. *Seizure Management*

It is important to know if a person is subject to seizures and to be prepared to handle the situation.

1. Remain calm and explain to others what is occurring. Others need to know that it is not contagious or something to fear.
2. Do not try to restrain the individual. Help the person to a comfortable position in a chair or onto the floor.
3. Remove all hazards in the area so that the person does not injure himself.
4. Turn the person's head sideways so that the airway is clear. Place a soft object under his head.
5. Do not force anything into the person's mouth.
6. Do not call for medical help unless the person has been injured or has repetitive seizures or seizures of a long duration.
7. Reassure the person and let him rest or sleep if he desires.
8. Do not pamper the person or allow him to rule the class or home because he has seizures.
9. Contact the parents or guardians if there has been an indication of seizure activity.
10. If you are responsible for a person with epilepsy, be sure you know his medication schedule.

F. *Cerebral Palsy*

Another condition characteristic of some mentally retarded persons is cerebral palsy. CP may be referred to as Little's Disease or congenital spastic paralysis. *Palsy* refers to a lack of control over the muscles and *cerebral* refers to the brain. Because of damage to the brain, the person is characterized by paralysis or muscle weakness, lack of coordination, motor impairment, speech deficits and sensory (ears, eyes, touch) difficulties.

Since cerebral palsy is caused by damage to the brain, a CP person may be mentally retarded. It should be noted that the presence of CP does not automatically mean that the person will be mentally retarded.

The CP person requires a variety of special helps in order to develop and maximize his ability to learn and live in society.

3

PROBLEMS CAUSED
BY MENTAL RETARDATION

T he birth of a retarded child introduces a complex structure of reactions, emotions, and problems to the parents, their families and friends as well as to the society into which the child is born. Each person involved may react in very diverse and complex ways.

A. *Parents' initial problems*

The news that their newborn child is retarded may be met with a large variety of emotions or reactions on the part of the parents. In fact, over fifty separate ones have been identified (Payne and Patton, 1981). Some parents are shocked or stunned, others grief-stricken or broken-hearted, while some become overwhelmed with depression or despair. They may feel isolated from loved ones and friends at a time when they desperately need the understanding and support of those closest to them.

Long time dreams and plans suddenly lay shattered in a crib where their retarded child sleeps. At the same time, parents may be depressed about their disappointment, guilty about their responsibility, angry about the injury done to them, and unsure about the meaning of this crisis as well as anxious about the child's future.

The first reaction may be disbelief. Sometimes the parents are unwilling to accept the diagnosis, which leads them to shop around for a different diagnosis; this never resolves the real problem. The parents may assume that the child is merely slow in developing or that he will soon outgrow the problem. They somehow believe that ignoring the problem will cause it to vanish.

It is not uncommon for the parents to express a sense of shame or to harbor many feelings of guilt or grief. Few who have the problem have not at some time asked, "Why us?" The parents may expect pity or ridicule and feel that family and friends look upon them as inferior. A severe loss of self-respect may also be involved. It is devastating to one's ego to have to admit that he has a defective child. Such feelings may lead to overindulgence or overprotection of the child.

Parents are frequently defensive and sensitive to criticism either expressed or implied. A slighting look, wrong gesture, or thoughtless comment often adds to the problem. Resentments may also build up toward the child or even toward others who do not face the same problem. Resentment can trigger depression or even hurt attitudes. Some parents assume a martyr complex and thus abandon themselves to the care of their child, often to the neglect of each other and other children in their family. The result is much family tension and problems between parents and their children.

B. *The problem of society*

Society's rejection of all that is not normal often results in unkind attitudes and actions toward the retarded and their families. As a result, society is very insensitive to their needs. Society implies that parents of retarded children should be "super parents" who are able to cope successfully with all the stress and act adequately in any situation that may arise.

A suspicious stare, skeptical attitude, unkind word, pointing out of the retarded person to others, and laughter when the child misbehaves or does not act his age appropriately, as well as social isolation, often cut deeply and cause great hurt or withdrawal. Parents and family members become overly concerned about what others will think and say and how the retarded person will act in public. They also have an obvious concern about how to deal with those who speak offensively about their retarded child. All too often the "professionals and friends" to whom a family turns for help tend to talk down to parents in a professional, patronizing, and authoritarian manner. They often lack tact or common sense and try to make decisions for the family. The family, however, requires a proper communication of truth in a loving and understandable manner so that they can make proper conclusions and decisions for themselves. They need to know what the alternatives are and the facts that must be considered. There are really no easy answers to the needs and problems families face in caring for their retarded children. No honest person working in the field of special education would presume to have all the answers. When seeking help and counsel, the parents need to be treated with dignity and respect. All too often parents are not allowed to talk and are censured for what they feel or say. Christians and the family's pastor should realize the need to give effective support, personal counsel, and practical help. Parents need to know that someone really cares, is interested in them and prays for them. Scripture demands that we "bear one another's burden" (Gal. 6:2), and that we be "doers of the Word, and not hearers only" (James 1:22). Unless the church family is supportive, the family life may be one of loneliness and constant strain.

C. *The problem of care*

Sooner or later the attention of the parents will begin to focus on the needs of their retarded child or adult. The problem of caring for a retarded individual is real and can only be fully realized by those who have faced the problem firsthand. The more severe the physical and mental handicap, the greater the problems the parents must face.

Parents must bear the responsibility of twenty-four-hour care for a child who demands more care and attention than the other family members. In addition, there are trips and time spent securing the necessary medical, educational, vocational, or support services outside of the home. The burden of care is also increased by the effect that the retarded individual has on other family members, neighbors, the church, and the community.

Another area of direct concern are the increased financial demands necessary to provide the needed level of care.

In exhaustion and desperation, the parents may ask, "What do we do now?" Only the parents have the God-given right and responsibility to make decisions concerning the care or placement of their child. The parents and family should not be pressured into making a decision that they may look at later with deep feelings of regret and guilt.

In making decisions concerning the care of a retarded person, a variety of factors must be taken into consideration. These may include:

1. The special educational, medical, vocational and custodial needs of the retarded individual
2. The severity of the individual's mental and physical handicaps
3. The health and age of the parents
4. The physical, emotional, and mental stress experienced by the other family members
5. The ability of the family to provide the required level of care
6. The availability of professional services in the local community
7. The importance of total programming (educational, vocational, spiritual, physical) and care in a Christian and Biblical setting
8. Is placement outside the home best for the individual and his family?

9. Is the decision prompted or motivated by the negative feelings or attitudes of the parents, family, or community?
10. Is the child's behavior causing injury to himself or others, or the destruction of personal and family property?

The decision to place a child outside of the home is an extremely difficult one. The pressures and factors involved can be appreciated only by those who have faced such a decision. Such placement outside of the home is an exception rather than the rule (Stubblefield, 1963). There are no cut-and-dried recipes or rules of thumb that cover every situation. Since no one factor will ultimately determine the decision, the Christian family should seek the Lord's will before making a decision. The options for other placement decisions are:

1. Staying at home with outside programming during the day
2. Foster home
3. Community living residence or group home
4. Semi-independent apartment complex
5. Residential school or training facility
6. Institution

Residential placement of the mentally retarded is no panacea! In fact, it may create more problems for the person and his family than it presumably cures. **No residential home or institution can ever replace a good *natural* home.** There is no substitute for the love and affection of one's own parents and family. However, a residential placement may offer a consistent program designed to meet the individual's needs that is difficult to provide in his own home. Routine is well established and discipline is maintained, and these are often what the retarded individual really needs.

More individualized and specialized care is also available to help the individual develop to his fullest potential in an environment geared to meet these demands. Trying to compete with normal peers is an ever-present problem. In a sense, the retarded person is living in a world made for him and inhabited by others like him. If the residential facility is a Christian home, more positive happy experiences are given.

Placing a retarded person outside of the home to forget the problems is impossible, for God has given man a memory. Such placement can lead to tragic ends for both the individual and his parents. Too many retarded persons reside in institutions soon to be forgotten by their parents and families. Don't underestimate the feelings of the retarded; they know when people really care!

The Christian who has the opportunity to counsel with the family of a retarded child or adult should avoid telling the parents what to do. *Remember!* This is a family decision that must be made after a consideration of all the factors involved and a determination of God's will. The parents and family need comfort, instruction, counsel and help to assist them in making correct and effective decisions. Such support and counsel is needed before and after they make a placement or care decision.

D. *Problem of educational or vocational training*

Parental expectations and hopes often far exceed the potential of the child or the services that are available. In spite of public awareness and the "free and appropriate education law," parents have difficulty in placing their child in the proper educational/vocational/residential programs. Further complications result because of different philosophies and levels of services available from area to area and state to state. For Christians, the problem is even more complex because of the desire for services that would not negate their spiritual convictions and training but would meet the total needs of their child.

E. *The discipline problem*

Contrary to public opinion, poor behavior is not synonymous with mental retardation. All too often, the retarded child is expected to be undisciplined, or is not disciplined on the grounds that he does not know any better. **Permissiveness or overprotection are perhaps the two major problems involved in the behavior patterns of the mentally retarded.** Parents, beset with guilt feelings and anxiety, sometimes tend to compensate by allowing the child to do as he pleases instead of taking disciplinary action. Frequently parents and family members attempt to do too much for the child, thus making him totally dependent and demanding. As a result, the child demands more and more time and attention from the parents instead of learning to act independently and caring for himself. The child needs adequate and loving discipline. Principles of discipline are considered in chapter 21.

F. *Problems for the Church*

On Sunday morning, a group of retarded young people may come to your church from a group home in your community. As the young people walk down the aisles and take their places in the pews, some church members may consider that their privacy is being invaded. The retarded young people may talk out loud, leave the service several times to go to the restoom or to get a drink, sing loudly or off key, drop money, etc. You may be offended by the affection they display as they shake your hand inappropriately. Some worshippers may react in fear and ultimately reject the retarded as individuals. In fact, some church members, due to prejudice, may communicate directly that the retarded and their families are not welcome at their church (Huff, 1981). Your church may find itself reacting like other churches in placing a limit on the number of retarded they will accept in their midst

(Racine [Wisconsin] Journal Times, May 31, 1980). What should the church do? How should its members react? What should be their response to the problems of mental retardation? Most retarded and their families do not attend church (Hawley, 1978). Obviously, some have been hurt and offended as a result of their contact with the church.

A survey of the church's role in programming for the mentally retarded will quickly indicate that there is a lot that is necessary to be done. This local church has the responsibility to:

1. Accept the retarded and his family
2. Help and counsel the family
3. Program in a meaningful way in order to win them to the Lord and disciple them in the Word of God

Section Two

OUR RESPONSIBILITY TO THE MENTALLY RETARDED

When we realize a need and see an opportunity, we automatically assume an obligation or responsibility to meet the need and fulfill the responsibility. God has chosen the family and the local church as the means to meet the spiritual needs of a lost and dying world . . . a world that includes the mentally retarded.

This section focuses upon . . .

The responsibility and concern that the local church should have for the mentally retarded

The opportunities that a pastor has for ministry to the mentally retarded and their families

Therefore to him that knoweth to do good,
and doeth it not, to him it is sin (James 4:17).

Where there is no vision, the people perish:
but he that keepeth the law,
happy is he (Prov. 29:18).

4

THE RESPONSIBILITY
OF THE CHURCH

The **mentally retarded** and their families still represent a vast mission field—a mission field that has not been reached for the Lord Jesus Christ. The Biblical mandate of the Church is to take the gospel message to every man in every part of the world, to make disciples, to equip for the ministry, and to send forth messengers into the harvest field (Matt. 28:18–20; Mark 16:15; Acts 1:8; Eph. 4:11, 12).

The church is more than a magnificent edifice or the people in attendance at a service of worship. The true measure of a church is the degree to which the church ministers to its community and to the uttermost part of the world. The local church is responsible for ministering to all people regardless of their human need, degree of suffering, or the level of their ability to respond. Therefore, the church should be concerned about mental retardation and its consequences for the individual, his family, the church and the community. "By ignoring the mentally retarded, the church has allowed the religion of humanism to catch the ear of both the retarded and their families" (Krental, 1981). How the church feels toward the retarded and their families counts more than what the church says or does (Stubblefield, 1965).

The importance of a ministry to the retarded is outlined in the following:

Bear ye one another's burdens,
and so fulfil the law of Christ (Gal. 6:2).

. . . comfort the feebleminded, support the weak,
be patient toward all men (1 Thess. 5:14).

33

> . . . *Inasmuch as ye have done it*
> *unto one of the least of these my brethren,*
> *ye have done it unto me (Matt. 25:40).*

Areas of Responsibility

1. *Conduct a comprehensive program* to meet the needs of the mentally retarded and their families. Such a program would differ only in degree, not in kind, from the regular program of the church (Stubblefield, 1965). Thus the Christian education program for the retarded is integrally related to the regular educational ministry of the church. The various aspects of such a program are considered in other chapters.

2. *Present an attitude of love, compassion and acceptance* to those who are characterized by rejection and failure. The mentally retarded should understand that they are accepted by the church just as any others who attend the church.

3. *Reach out, support, and sustain* those who have special needs because of the problem of mental retardation. Words of encouragement and deeds of concern and care are needed from everyone, not just the pastor. The families of the retarded need to have contact with others so that they can express their concerns without apology.

4. *Provide literature* in the field of mental retardation. The literature may be books that can be checked out of the church library, books or booklets left with the family at the time of initial contact, or a source list of available information.

5. *Involve the parents* in the planning of programs to meet the special needs of the retarded.

6. *Provide training courses or seminars* designed to address areas of parental need and concern such as childrearing problems, social adjustment, developmental needs, discipline, or spiritual training.

7. *Provide assistance* in caring for the needs of the retarded child so that the parents can attend church, enjoy an outing, take a trip, etc. (See the respite section in chapter 13.) Parents often do not attend services because of the embarrassment of having a retarded child, or the level of care necessary does not allow them to bring the child to church. Stubblefield (1965) refers to a family who welcomed help because they had not been able to attend a church or Sunday School for five years.

8. *Provide information* to the total church family about mental retardation. In ignorance and fear, too many church members refuse to be physically close to a retarded person and his family or to visit in the home.

The responsibility of ministering to the spiritual needs of the retarded and their families must be accepted by the local church. Because of the presence of a retarded child, hearts may be open and tender. The family needs help to maintain or find personal faith in a loving and caring God.

In dealing with the retarded and their families, our responsibility before the Lord is to be a faithful witness. The results must be left in His hands. Suggestions for leading a retarded person to Christ are found in chapter 20.

5

THE RESPONSIBILITY
OF THE PASTOR

The initial contact with the family may be the responsibility of the pastor. Contrary to the opinion of some pastors, the pastor should not wait until he is asked to visit (Stubblefield, 1965). Various responses and conflicts may prohibit the family from contacting the pastor or having any contact with the church. At such a time of stress and problems, the presence and counsel of a pastor are needed.

The pastor has the opportunity to:

1. Provide support for the family by helping them to recognize and accept their retarded child

2. Help the parents and family to clarify their thoughts and to pinpoint specific problem areas for which help can be secured

3. Counsel and strengthen the family whose faith and trust may be shattered at the birth of a retarded child

4. Present Biblical truth concerning exceptionalities to the family (i.e., Exod. 4:11; Lev. 19:14; John 9:3)

5. Encourage the family to maintain or establish regular attendance and participation in the fellowship and services of the church

6. Provide supportive and informational literature for the parents

7. Assist the family in securing the help of community and professional agencies and services that the family may need. Be sure the church provides supportive services

8. Encourage the family to take their retarded child to church with them and to participate in the church's programming for the mentally retarded

9. Enlist church members to help the family, through fellowship, meals, babysitting, etc.

10. Maintain a continual warm and supportive ministry and relationship that will help the family to feel accepted in the midst of a caring church fellowship

11. Lead the church in establishing a ministry for the mentally retarded covering all aspects of the church

12. Counsel with the retarded person at times of decision in his life, i.e., conversion, baptism, program enrollment, schooling, etc.

Once we begin to understand some of the problems parents face, we can begin to consider ways of offering them the help and consideration they need. Always bear in mind the importance of *not giving authoritative advice* in areas rightfully belonging to a psychiatrist, psychologist, doctor or other professional persons.

The Christian worker's task is to help the family maintain or find faith in God. Perhaps their faith has faltered and they need it restored. Spiritual help in time of trouble is the only real answer. Give it with love and compassion, remembering that unless we have passed through the same waters, we don't really know what our reactions would be.

Let the family know that you care. Alert your own family and friends or the congregation to the problem of mental retardation. Compassionate concern communicates itself to parents! After all, what is in the heart speaks to the heart and parents can discern genuine interest. Remember that they have been deeply hurt.

Remember, too, that there is no easy answer to the needs of families faced with this problem. Avoid advice! Don't tell them what you'd do but rather point out alternatives. They must make their own decisions and then live with them. Undergird them with your prayer support. Help them to get busy doing something about their problems instead of sitting around questioning. The secret may be "How can we take what has happened to our family and use it to God's glory?"

What is unknown in this field overshadows the known. There is no set answer to "Why did this happen to us?" Don't attempt to answer this question for in reality we have no right to question God's doings. Verses of comfort like James 1:5 and Romans 8:28 will give peace as they think about the future.

When counseling the family, treat them with dignity and respect. Let them talk and express whatever feelings they wish. Don't censure them for expressing what they do. Be honest and fair with them. Above all else, listen to them. They may reveal much that will help you deal with their problems. Be positive in discussing the probable future of the child. Talk in terms of success and what may be achieved instead of what failures they may meet. Give them hope!

Section Three

ORGANIZING A CHURCH PROGRAM FOR THE MENTALLY RETARDED

Having established the need for a ministry to the retarded in the local church and having completed a thorough review of the causes and characteristics of mental retardation, the tedious but enjoyable task of organization begins. At this point, careful and prayerful consideration needs to be given to each detail to ensure the best possible beginning for the ministry with the retarded. The success and growth of this ministry may well be determined by the degree of organization and planning prior to and during the implementation of this program. Dependence upon God cannot be overemphasized. It is absolutely essential!

Trust in the LORD with all thine heart;
and lean not unto thine own understanding.
In all thy ways acknowledge him,
and he shall direct thy paths (Prov. 3:5, 6).

Let all things be done decently and in order (1 Cor. 14:40).

6

MEETING THE LOCAL NEED

Each church and community will differ in the number of mentally retarded in its midst. (A good rule of thumb is 3% of the population of the community.) Any program, therefore, should also appeal to families who are not a part of the church's sphere of ministry. The estimation of a potential enrollment is necessary for (1) adequate planning of the type of program, (2) determination of program priorities, (3) recruitment of the needed staff and (4) determination of space and equipment needs.

Contacts for enrollment in the church's program may be gained from several sources. It is important to make friendly contacts with parents and professionals who are involved in the field of special education. Although laws prohibit the sharing of certain information, you may be able to make contact with or get literature to potential prospects through such contacts. Potential enrollment contacts may be gained through:

1. Members of your church or Sunday School, from pulpit, bulletin and assembly announcements
2. Prospect letters and questionnaires given to participants in the various programs of the church
3. Congregational families who have retarded family members
4. Current public or private special education programs in the community such as schools, sheltered workshops, group homes and day care programs
5. Attendance at meetings of local units of the NARC (National Association for Retarded Citizens)
6. Attendance at any special education functions in the community
7. Visitation program in your community including cradle roll calls,

families who have retarded family members, newcomers to the community and a door-to-door canvas

8. Contact with medical and educational professionals
9. Promotion through notices or advertisements on radio, TV, newspaper, church bulletins, brochures for general distribution, or bulk mailing flyers and posters in stores
10. Contacts with children

Depending upon the size of the church and community and program priorities, the search for prospects may involve several stages or levels as well as being a continuous enrollment program. An initial survey may be helpful in establishing a preview of the potential need.

Once a potential for enrollment has been established, plans should be made for staff recruitment and training and any final promotion necessary to meet the determined need.

The information gained in the enrollment survey process also will be helpful in establishing priorities in the type and level of program to be launched (see chapter 7).

How many retarded individuals are needed to start a class? One individual may become the nucleus of your program. One retarded child in a Sunday School constitutes a class (Wood, 1961; Hahn and Raasch, 1969).

Church Programming

As noted previously, church programming for the mentally retarded should be an integral part of the total church ministry. Thus, it is not a different kind of a program except in degree, content, methods and emphasis. The program for the mentally retarded will include the same program elements that the church maintains for everyone else.

A church should not try to include the mentally retarded in all of its program elements at one time. Since very few of the retarded are ready, it is recommended that you begin with the Sunday School and then expand to include other programs one at a time.

In initial planning, the church leadership will have to make decisions concerning how the program will relate to the other church ministries. In preliminary planning, there is no easy solution to estimate the type of needed program structure, since the needs of those who will be enrolled are not known. The three basic program designs are (1) a separate program, either in the church or in a group home, (2) an integrated program where the retarded participate in existing programs and (3) a combination where the retarded are in separate programs and integrated into other programs (i.e., integrated in opening exercises or first part of worship service and then separated for the lesson period).

The following factors need to be considered in order to make such decisions:

1. *The Enrollment*—Basic to planning and program decisions is a determination of a potential enrollment. Each church and community will differ in the number of mentally retarded children in its midst as well as the severity of mental handicaps. The program also will have appeal to families who may not be part of the church's ministry sphere. Through a pre-enrollment process, information would be secured as to a potential number, classification or degree of retardation, presence or absence of speech, and degree of physical disability or limitation. For example: a group of mildly retarded adults might be included in the regular worship service following a time of orientation and readiness training whereas a group of trainable children might be best served in a separate program.

The information gained concerning potential enrollment would also be valuable when making decisions concerning space and number of staff to be recruited.

2. *Available Space*—A consideration of the availability of space establishes the direction a church may take. Limited space may dictate that a separate program like a Sunday School class during the morning worship service is necessary. It also could indicate that provision should be made for additional building space so that such a program could be possible.

3. *Community mental retardation education and program philosophy* may also be an important factor. The philosophy of complete integration is very strong in some areas. In many instances, the parents are the impetus and support of such programming. In such instances, it may not be wise to consider a separate program without a parent, church and community readiness program.

4. *Available Leadership*—The experience and number of staff that is available are also important factors to consider. Inexperienced staff, for example, may be more at ease working in a separate program. There also may not be enough experienced staff available to work with a number of small groups. As one gains knowledge of the retarded and practical experience working with them, it becomes easier to adapt and integrate a program. Many regular staff possibly would resist efforts to have the mentally retarded placed in their regular classes.

Ultimately, the needs of the mentally retarded should be most important in making program decisions. An effective program will meet their needs. Placement with consideration of one's mental age, physical size, social and emotional maturity is essential.

5. *Program Elements*—A variety of program ministries for the mentally retarded need to be considered by the church leadership. These ministries not only provide for the needs of the mentally retarded as individuals but

also offer a potential outreach to their families. Suggestions for implementing these programs are found in a number of later chapters.

Possible program ministries are:

a. Sunday School
b. Worship services
c. Christian day school classes
d. Home Bible study classes
e. Youth and club programs
f. Daily vacation Bible school
g. Social and recreational
h. Camping
i. Personal devotions helps
j. Adoptive grandparents
k. Respite and day care ministries
l. Transportation
m. Group homes
n. Sheltered workshops

Programs should be considered to meet the needs of both children and adults. The groupings within each area will be dependent upon the number who are involved and the degree of their handicaps.

7

LAUNCHING A MINISTRY
TO THE RETARDED

A ministry to the mentally retarded should not be undertaken without adequate preparation, which includes a consideration of all aspects of the church's total ministry. Success comes by allowing the Lord to plan your work and then working the plan.

Based on Proper Motivation

The first basic step is to analyze why the program is being undertaken. There should be a realistic basis for undertaking such a program.

1. The purpose is not to set up a diagnostic or clinical department for the study of mentally retarded individuals. This does not preclude that the church's special education staff may not have diagnostic training or experience or may not do any testing or diagnosis.

2. The program should not be launched out of pity or because of an underlying sense of individual or group guilt. A successful program cannot be based upon pity for the plight of mentally retarded individuals.

3. A church should not be pressured into establishing a program because of the parents, or because of a few individuals in the church or the community.

4. There should be no spirit of competition or of "keeping up with the Joneses."

5. The program should be undertaken to minister to the spiritual needs of the retarded and their families.

The church should have clearly defined Scriptural goals or reasons for launching a special education program. This program should be an integral part of the church's total program and should be designed to meet the basic needs of the mentally retarded. It should be moved by Christian love and launched with a sense of God-given responsibility and direction.

Who Should Do the Planning

Anyone may be used of God as the catalyst for launching a special education program in the church. When God is at work, He will place a burden on a pastor, deacon, parent, Sunday School worker, etc. This individual will begin to share his burden with the pastor and others by enlisting prayer support or involvement. Those who are interested will merge into a group of concerned Christians. From the beginning, the desire and plan should be to **work through the organizational structure of the church so that the program will not exist as a separate entity.**

Since the pastor has a God-given responsibility for the total ministry of the church, his advice and support should be sought and obtained from the start. You may want to study carefully the church's organizational structure, the field of mental retardation and what is now being done in programing for the mentally retarded. Together a plan will develop in relation to the proper procedure for working with the boards, committees, etc., that are responsible for such a ministry. The steps taken would then be directed by local church procedures. In most churches, the ultimate decision will rest with the congregation who would be asked to approve, finance and become involved.

Planning the Work—Working the Plan!

Let all things be done decently and in order (1 Cor. 14:40).

Do not rush to get a program started. To avoid problems within the local church assembly, it is essential to begin the ministry slowly and to spend much time in prayer and careful planning.

Since mental retardation and the mentally retarded are not understood by most individuals, a congregational readiness program should be considered. Such a program is designed to introduce and prepare the congregation for the ministry in providing information about the nature and characteristics of mental retardation, the needs of the mentally retarded and what Shepherds and other local churches are doing for them. This program could include:
1. Films
2. Books, pamphlets and other miscellaneous literature
3. The ministry of a gospel team from Shepherds
4. Slide presentation of Shepherds

   5. Field visits to Shepherds and to other local church programs
   6. Displays
   7. Pastoral messages
   8. Informational and/or discussion meetings

The planning stage should include:
   1. Local church approval and support
   2. Surveying the church and community need (See chapter 6.)
   3. Defining priorities as to the program elements (See chapters 6, 10, 11, 12, 13, 22.)
   4. Establishing rules and regulations (See chapter 8.)
   5. Enlisting and training workers (See chapter 9.)
   6. Determining a budget
   7. Allocation of space
   8. Securing necessary equipment and supplies
   9. Transportation
  10. Student enrollment
  11. Establishing a target date for beginning
  12. Visitation of prospects and absentees
  13. Evaluation and expansion to other program possibilities

The overall plan should ultimately provide that:
   1. The retarded will know through attitude and action that they are loved and accepted within the local church.
   2. Adequate staff has been enlisted and trained
   3. Families and parents will be welcome
   4. The church will approve and support the program

8

GENERAL GUIDELINES

Aims/Objectives

The aims or objectives of a church's ministry to the mentally retarded are directly related to the total aim and objective of a local church. Because of the characteristics and limitations of mental retardation certain aims or objectives become important. The overall aims can be further broken down into a larger list of specific instructional or program objectives and lesson aims.

The mentally retarded need:

1. To accept Jesus Christ as their own personal Savior
2. To know and understand that the Bible as God's Word tells us how to obey, live for and please God
3. To develop spiritually to their full potential
4. To relate Biblical truth to concrete, life-changing situations
5. To learn to honor, respect, love and serve God
6. To participate in the programs of the local church
7. To know and practice appropriate social and independent living skills
8. To gain self-confidence and self-worth through successful life experiences
9. To learn to be a vehicle of witness and ministry to their families
10. To know that others care for, love and respect them as people who are important to God and His people
11. To respect those in places of authority
12. To study and memorize God's Word

Of necessity, these goals cannot be accomplished at one time or in one particular program, but through patient and loving care and instruction over a long period of time. There will be varying degrees of success depending upon the degree of retardation and resultant limitations of each individual.

Guidelines and Regulations

Once the aims and objectives have been settled upon, the local church should not overlook the importance of establishing general guidelines and regulations for its special educational programming. Guidelines will aid in dealing with problems and avoiding conflicts or misunderstandings. Since there may be differences of viewpoint in some areas, it is important to clarify and agree on issues before a program is launched. Some guidelines or regulations may vary in accord with the preferences and priorities of the local church and its leadership.

Some problem areas that should be covered are:

1. *Those who are to be enrolled*—This should cover areas such as: (a) what prerequisite skills are necessary? (b) will we accept only those in our church family? (c) must they be toilet trained? (d) will we provide a children's program? (e) will we provide an adult program? (f) will we accept only those currently enrolled in a special education program? (g) will we limit the program to mildly or moderately retarded? (h) must they have some speech and language abilities? (i) will we allow discipline or behavior problems? (j) will we begin with a limited number to start?

2. *Type of Program Groupings*—Includes areas such as chronological age, mental age, handicap level, class size, separate classes, integrated program.

3. *Parents* will not be in the class with their child but hopefully in an appropriate Sunday School class for their own needs.

4. *Transportation*—Who will provide? Will there be any cost, etc.?

5. *Discipline Code*—Covering areas such as What is it? How should it be enforced? When will discipline be used?

6. *Behavior or Conduct Code*—Covering areas such as dress, swearing and smoking

7. *Complaint Procedure*—If child/adult has problems and relates them to parents, call teacher for clarification.

8. *Visitors*

9. *Offering*

10. *Take Home Literature*—Communication with parents

11. *Insurance and Liability*—On premises and on field trips

12. *Medical and Emergency Procedures*—Particularly important if any students have seizures

9

RECRUITING AND TRAINING QUALIFIED WORKERS

It **is generally** recognized that the teacher or leader is the key in helping the retarded to learn. Thus **the success or failure of the church's special education program lies in the selection of its teachers and leaders.** Very few people possess all the desirable characteristics outlined below. This should not discourage participation because God is able to make us to be "approved workmen" if we are willing to trust Him. However, evaluation of one's self in relation to these desirable characteristics is important. It will reveal the areas where progress is needed. Not all people who love God and desire to serve Him will be able to work with the mentally retarded.

Teacher Characteristics and Qualifications

The first and most important area of concern should be the spiritual qualifications and characteristics of prospective teachers and leaders. The qualifications would be the same as the spiritual qualifications for workers found in the Word of God and outlined by the local church. Added to these would be appropriate personal and professional qualities. Someone has said that a lot of what is involved in working with the mentally retarded is basic common sense and good educational practice.

An effective leader/teacher of the retarded will be:

1. A person who knows Christ as his personal Savior
2. A person who has a consistent and godly testimony and walk
3. A person who is familiar with the characteristics of the mentally retarded and willing to become knowledgeable by reading and being involved in leadership training classes

4. A person who is able to accept the mentally retarded as people for whom Christ died and a person who is interested in associating with them and loving them

5. A person who is patient and gentle, yet firm in conviction, with the ability to function as an authority figure in the role of leadership

6. A person who is able to accept individuals as they are but with the vision to see what they may become in the Lord

7. A person with a creative and resourceful attitude, able to create as well as adapt materials, lessons, etc., and one who can cope with the constant repetition and the slow progress the retarded will make

8. A humble and persistent person who is willing to trust the Lord and not give up easily

9. A person who is physically and emotionally able to cope with the teaching demands

10. One who is able to remain objective and adjust to any situation

11. A person with a good sense of humor

12. An active and mature member of the local church

The mentally retarded will know whether their teacher or leader is interested in them and accepts them in love, not pity or sympathy. If you are not willing to hear them, why should they listen to you when you speak?

Recruiting Workers

Although not essential, it is obviously an advantage to have workers in the local church who have training and experience in working with the mentally retarded. The recruitment process should begin by looking for those who have experience and training in the church's educational programs—Sunday School teachers, school teachers, special education teachers, etc. College young people, adult fellowships and grandparents' clubs are also possible areas of recruitment.

When the need for workers has been made known, careful and prayerful consideration is necessary before possible workers are individually approached. The potential training programs should be intact so that they can be shared with prospective workers. Experienced workers in the field of Christian education of the retarded warn against using parents of the retarded in such programs because of their close emotional involvement with the children (Wood, 1961; Hahn & Raasch, 1969). The parents also need time to be refreshed spiritually in study and fellowship with other believers. Teachers and staff members should be selected in light of the many factors that are of concern in the total programming for the mentally retarded.

Teacher/pupil ratios in programs for the mentally retarded should be kept small. The specific needs and abilities of those who are enrolled will serve as a guide in determining the exact number of workers needed. A minimum of two workers is needed if more than one member is enrolled. Staff ratios may vary from one to one in a group of severely retarded, to one to five or six in a mildly retarded group.

Separate programs would require more staff than those with various degrees of integration into already existing programs.

Training Workers

Because the ministry to the mentally retarded is specialized, the provision of a training program is important to the enrollment and preparation of staff. Prospective workers may be obtained more easily if they can be assured of preservice training and inservice help and assistance. The training program should provide a basic knowledge and understanding of the characteristics and needs of the mentally retarded, principles of working with the retarded, organizational help and specific teaching and problem areas. A training program could include:

1. A study course in the *Introduction to Mental Retardation,* using an accepted overview text

2. A reading and discussion program to give information in the field of mental retardation

3. Workshops led by special education staff from public or Christian schools

4. Field trips to other church or school programs for the retarded

5. Attending conferences and meetings conducted by local educational agencies, American Association on Mental Deficiency, Council for Exceptional Children and the National Association for Retarded Citizens

6. Serve as an aide in a program

7. Work with a retarded person in a home setting, or in a program as a tutor or teacher's aide

8. Films and videotapes on mental retardation

9. Courses in mental retardation at a nearby college

10. Preservice training classes

11. Institute an aide training program whereby new staff work with other staff when they are interested in the ministry to the retarded

12. Attendance at a summer session of Shepherds College of Special Education

10

STARTING A SUNDAY SCHOOL PROGRAM

An ideal program with which to begin is a Sunday School program because (a) it is a basic program in most churches, (b) it is easily adapted to meet the needs of a few or many and (c) one mentally retarded child in a Sunday School constitutes the basis for a class. Although a church may launch a Sunday School program to meet the specific need of one or a few, plans should be made for expansion and outreach to other mentally retarded in the community.

Steps in Starting a Sunday School Program

1. Survey the immediate need in the local church
2. Secure the support of the church and Sunday School leadership
3. Survey the community need and locate prospects
4. Determine the organizational structure of the classes—adults or children, separated or integrated, rules and regulations
5. Allocate space for the class(es)
6. Enlist and train the needed workers
7. Select curriculum, supplies, and equipment
8. Arrange for necessary transportation services
9. Determine the starting date
10. Establish a visitation program for new prospects (before the program actually begins) and for follow-up

Scope of the Sunday School Program

In the planning, decisions will have to be made concerning the various aspects of the church's ministry to the mentally retarded through the Sunday School. Such decisions will be made in part on the basis of the immediate church need, community prospects, available staff, appropriate space and church administrative preferences or policy.

Sunday School classes may be held for children or adults, or they may be limited to a particular classification group. Nursery type services for the severely retarded may also be necessary so that their families can attend an appropriate class.

Should there be separate Sunday School classes for the retarded or should they be integrated into the regular classes? Such a decision is not always easy to make but should be made on the basis of local need and the best interest of those who are to attend (see the principles outlined in chapter 8). The Sunday School program for the retarded may have immediate and long range stages and include various types of separate or integrated or combinations of the two. Priorities may be established by considering the number of pupils, ability levels, individual needs, available room space and the experience and capabilities of available leadership.

When Should the Class Meet?

If at all possible, the class, as an integral part of the Sunday School, should meet during the regular Sunday School hour. In this way, the class or classes for the mentally retarded are not isolated from the total Sunday School program nor regarded as something "different." In addition, having the class as part of the regular Sunday School program encourages and makes it possible for the parents and other family members to attend.

If the present facilities are already taxed to the limit of space, it may be necessary for the Sunday School class to meet during the morning worship hour or at another time during the day.

Sunday School classes could also be held in nursing homes, group homes, residential institutions, or training schools. Such classes would meet at times mutually acceptable to the leadership of the church and the organization involved.

Classroom Location

Although other factors or priorities may determine such decisions, when selecting a classroom, be sure it is:
1. Accessible to entrances and easy to find
2. On the ground level to avoid complications with stairs

3. Located away from noise or distractions, if possible (Carpet and accoustical tile help.)
4. Attractive, neat, well-lighted, ventilated and a proper size for the group
5. Close to restrooms
6. Their own room, not a part of another classroom with a divider

A Sunday School Readiness Program

Adults or children who have never been active in a Sunday School class will require all the basic readiness skills taught in the nursery-beginner departments of the Sunday School. These objectives (readiness skills) are those referred to as "Learning to Worship God," or "Behavior in God's House." These objectives include the following:

1. Taking care of one's possessions

Depending upon their background, many of the children or adults will need to be taught where and how to hang up their coats and put away other belongings. Be sure they do not come to class still wearing winter coats, boots, etc. Finding a centrally located coat area where not much traffic will congregate is advisable. Each Sunday (or for services during other parts of the week) they should be instructed to place their possessions in this location. Perhaps using a teenager or parent to assist in this area, especially in winter, would be helpful since it would free the teacher for the classroom. Within the class, assign places to store possessions brought to class when they are not using them. Doing so will prevent the pupils from playing with articles and will lessen distractions.

2. Locating a chair and remaining in it

Teaching the child or adult to locate a chair and remain in it during the Bible lesson is difficult at first. He may have a tendency to get up and sit by his friends, or wander around the room. Don't be afraid to be firm. Insist on his staying in the chair during the Bible lesson time but allow freedom to change during the activity time or other specific times. This concept will build toward the time when he is ready to sit with adults in the worship service or other selected programs.

3. Learning to listen

Have them place Bibles, purses, and other objects under their chairs. This will enable them to look directly at you while you are talking or presenting the Bible lesson and will discourage them from playing with their Bibles, turning pages, etc. When you use the Bible for verses, or when you use song books, help them to locate the reference or page and place a marker in the selection. Don't shout to them. Speak in a natural voice, low if necessary to get their attention. Remind them that only you can speak during the service unless you ask for their help. When they do get loud, simply say, "I'm talking; please wait," or whatever is appropriate for the situation.

4. Music—learning to sing

The majority of students probably will not know the songs you want them to sing. Since they will want to please you, they will substitute noises instead of words. One way to avoid this and also provide for appropriate church behavior is to introduce the songs to them with the words. Teach them phrase by phrase so they can learn to sing the correct words. If they revert to noises, go over the words again. Some will not be able to learn the words but the majority will carry their voices with words above them. Remember also to stress that they do not have to sing loudly; softness with words produces music.

Class Schedule

A rigid type of schedule may look good in planning but may not always work out in practice. However, the class period should be well structured to insure a smoothly running program. **Routine and well-defined expectations and limits are a source of security for the mentally retarded.** The schedule should be flexible with individual time components structured to allow for change or for the unexpected. Possible schedule components are:

1. Welcome—take care of coats, boots, etc. Make visit to the restroom before class begins.
2. Interest Center and free time
3. Music and memory verse
4. Prayer and praise time
5. Announcements and offering
6. Bible story or lesson
7. Stretch and restroom break—*only if necessary and should be discouraged*
8. Handwork and expression time
9. Exercise and rest time
10. Closing and dismissal

A sample schedule is located in Appendices A and B.

Curriculum

The curriculum materials selected should fit the physical and mental age levels and spiritual needs of the individuals of the class. Curriculum guidelines are found in chapter 14. An annotated reference list of the Sunday School lessons available from Shepherds, Inc., is found in Appendix C.

Registration and Enrollment

Students should be enrolled by their parents or guardians. Such an enrollment may be completed during a visit in their home, during an enrollment day, or when the child or adult is brought to the first session of the Sunday School class. The enrollment should secure:

1. Name
2. Address
3. Date of birth
4. Parents'/guardians' name and address if different
5. Telephone number
6. Name of other family members
7. Church affiliation
8. Current church programming
9. Diagnosis and degree of retardation
10. Physical problems (visual, hearing, motor, seizures, toileting)
11. Behavioral problems (hitting, biting, kicking, tantrums)
12. Methods of control or discipline
13. How will they be transported? (List church bus or route number of the individual.)
14. Emergency information including medication
15. Registration observations of child/adult, parents, etc.
16. Parental signature
17. Where parent will be while you have the child/adult in your program

II

BEGINNING A
WORSHIP PROGRAM

Worship is a basic Scriptural and spiritual need of the mentally retarded just as it is of any other individual. Because of this assumption, it is not the purpose of this chapter to consider the nature of true Biblical worship but to consider guidelines for structuring a worship program for the mentally retarded.

Where Should the Retarded Worship?

Should the mentally retarded person worship with his family in the regular church worship services, with his peers, or in a separate worship service? The local church must answer these questions while developing its program, philosophy and plan. The following should be considered:

1. The elements of the regular worship service may be different or confusing for the retarded to understand.

2. Behavioral or physical characteristics may rule out participation in a regular service for such a long time or may indicate a need for participation in a readiness program for a period of time.

3. The degree of a person's mental and physical disablilty

4. The degree of other limitations

5. The desire of the congregation or board

6. The presence of selected adults to sponsor unaccompanied individuals by sitting with them

Mentally retarded persons need to and want to worship. Where and how they worship may depend upon decisions made in light of the above factors. The opinions of leaders differ in this area. No matter what decision is reached, if the intent is to teach spiritual truth, the material must be in line with the person's level of mental or intellectual functioning (mental age). The church should carefully consider all areas of the worship program before it is begun. Churches have been split over where and when the retarded should worship (*Rules on Retarded Stir Church Uproar,* Racine [Wisconsin] Journal Times, May 31, 1980). Some churches have prohibited participation on the part of mentally retarded individuals (*Not Smart Enough for Church,* Christianity Today, August 7, 1981).

A Worship Readiness Program

A readiness program to prepare the entire church body, as well as the mentally retarded who will participate, should be considered. The elements of preparing a congregation for a ministry to the retarded were considered in chapter 7. Proper information and communication are vital to the success of any program.

Initially, as you launch the program, it is essential to remember that a few selected individuals may participate in the regular morning, evening and midweek worship services. These individuals will function within the higher trainable or educable levels, have the necessary social skills so they will not offend the regular worshippers, and understand the Biblical truths addressed in the service. It must be remembered that not all mentally retarded will benefit from integration into the regular worship services. In these cases, a self-contained program will best meet their needs.

The following training program, as outlined, will be a gradual transition from the self-contained Sunday worship service to the sanctuary. The young people/adults will attend the regular service once a month then return to their classroom. In the following weeks, discussions will center around the positive and negative behaviors exhibited in the service until the individuals are ready to worship full time as part of the congregation. As noted in chapter 10, some of the program of worship readiness and training may also be necessary when a Sunday School class is started.

The room should be set up to resemble the church service. This includes such things as rows of chairs for pews, offering plate, hymn books, pulpit and a hymn board to list the hymns. In addition to the areas suggested in the Sunday School Readiness Program, (chapter 10), emphasize the following:

1. VISIT RESTROOM. To avoid confusion during the worship service, as well as distracting from the service, the students need to understand and remember to visit the restroom prior to entering the room. The instructor, at first, will need to remind individuals to do this every Sunday. Once the service has begun, the individuals should be expected to remain in their pew (seats) for at least one hour and fifteen minutes.

2. SELECTION OF A PEW. The first part of the service should be devoted to the selection of a pew. Emphasis is placed upon sitting in the middle of the pew if the seat is empty and, if partially filled, sitting toward the end. The hardest concept to teach is to not sit too close to friends in the pew when they go to church. Bring other people in to fill the chairs to give additional practice. Teaching the ability to locate a pew and remain in it during the service is difficult at first. The student may have a tendency to want to get up and sit by his friends, or wander around the room. Don't be afraid to be firm. Insist that he stay in the pew or chair during the service.

3. MUSIC— USE OF THE HYMNAL. Teach the first stanzas of the hymns used in the services; any particular closing songs, prayer songs, or choruses should also be taught. Teach the proper way to hold a hymnal—right side up—and how to open the book. If the church has a hymn board displaying the selections, have one in the room. Teach students to look up each hymn in advance to familiarize themselves with using a hymnal. Emphasize singing softly and not screaming when singing, as it hurts the ears of the people ahead of them. For specific music helps, see chapter 17.

4. PASSING OF THE OFFERING PLATE. Select two individuals to act as ushers. Pass plates from the aisle across the row to each individual. Depending upon the level of the adults, you may wish to teach them how to grasp the plates without money in them first. Later, add some weight to the plate so it will feel heavier. Emphasize the importance of listening and having their offering ready to place into the offering plate as it is passed. The use of offering envelopes should be encouraged. These should be prepared at home to avoid confusion at the time of the offering. Instruction should also be given that the offering is being given to God and His work. Share information as to how the offering is used in taking care of God's work.

5. MAKE A SAMPLE BULLETIN. List the order of the service on this. Mark when they are to stand up, remain seated, selection of Scriptures, etc. If possible, secure the church bulletins for that day and use them. At first, you will need to change the hymn selections because of the limited amount of songs they know.

6. PREACHING TIME. This is where you will have the Bible lesson for the day. Again, stress that during the worship time, they are to be quiet.

7. VISIT A SERVICE. Take them into the worship service for part of their church time. Leave the service during the singing of the last hymn before the message. Evaluate their progress with them. Praise them for their good points and go over things that need improving. After several times of following this procedure, allow them to go to the service for the entire period. **The ultimate goal of worship readiness is integration into the regular worship service for those capable of participating.**

Self-Contained Worship Services

Many of the mentally retarded who attend local church programs will not profit from the regular worship services. For them, a separate worship service conducted on their level and designed to meet their specific needs will be more effective. Integration into the regular worship services for special days or events may be a part of this program as well. A worship readiness program may be built into the self-contained program as you begin but should not be continued as a special emphasis, since the end goal will not be integration.

Almost all the elements of a regular worship service may be incorporated into the worship service for the mentally retarded, if there is careful planning designed to meet their individual and group needs. Of course, these components must be adapted to the mental age and functioning level of the worshipping group.

1. PRESERVICE. All leaders and helpers should arrive at least fifteen minutes early to care for all areas of preparation and to be ready to greet the worshippers as they arrive. This shows personal interest in the individual and allows the worshippers to communicate needs and desires. If the worshippers are coming directly from a Sunday School program, they should first visit the restroom. A special prayer bulletin board (including pictures, words, prayer requests, etc.) could be used to encourage prayerful meditation during the prelude.

2. PRELUDE. A musical prelude by a pianist, organist, or cassette tape will help the worshippers settle down and prepare for worship.

3. PRAYER. Prayer is an important aspect of the spiritual life of the mentally retarded. Training is needed not only in what prayer is but also in how to pray, including both instruction and practice. Leaders may also learn a lot about the needs and concerns of the retarded through the prayer times. Specific prayer helps are found in chapter 18.

4. SCRIPTURE READING. A central Scripture passage should be selected to set the theme for the service. The passage may be centered around the memory verse for the day. If possible, use one of the worshippers to participate in the Scripture reading. The passage should be selected in light of their ability to understand. Memory verse helps are given in chapter 18.

5. MUSIC. Retarded persons usually enjoy music and love to sing. Even the most severely retarded are able to respond to music even though they may not be able to read or to sing. The mildly retarded can learn both the words and the music. Biblical truths may be taught and reinforced through music. The music part of the worship service should provide an opportunity for the worshippers to participate as well as providing special music for their enjoyment. Youth and church musicians can serve as guest participants. If

the size and capabilities of the group permit, with some practical music training, a choir could be developed. Specific music helps are listed in chapter 17.

6. BIBLE LESSON (MESSAGE). It is suggested that this part of the service should take approximately one-fourth of the time available. The Bible lesson should deal with Biblical truths as they relate to the lives and needs of the retarded.

The materials selected for the presentation of the Bible lesson should be appropriate for the functional level of the group, adapted to meet their learning characteristics, and correlated with the other parts of the service.

Since the retarded individual learns by repetition, one lesson is taught for a minimum of four to six weeks. To assist you in thinking of a variety of methods, we have listed the following for your consideration:

  a. Short text presentation
  b. Group discussion for the application of the text selected
  c. Visualized Bible lesson
  d. Object lesson
  e. Drama or role playing
  f. Films and audio visual aids
  g. Puppets, ventriloquism
  h. Pictures

The Bible lesson time can also be used effectively with higher functioning individuals to prepare them for church membership, as well as to present Biblical instruction in church life and doctrine. Feature guest speakers, such as the pastor, a deacon or a missionary. Areas such as the following should be covered:

  a. The plan of salvation
  b. The local church
  c. Doctrinal statement of the local church
  d. Covenant of the local church
  e. Qualifications of church officers
  f. Duties of church officers
  g. Responsibilities of church members
  h. Church ordinances

The theme of the worship service may be correlated with the Shepherds Sunday School lesson series being used, as well as with the memory verse and review work. A list of available lesson series is found in Appendix C.

Note on church ordinances: The mentally retarded should not be excluded from baptism, church membership, and participation at the Lord's Supper just because they are retarded. Since these are areas of church responsibility, the church should establish procedures for these ordinances.

The mentally retarded applicant for baptism or church membership should be considered and processed just like any other applicant. They should meet with the pastor and deacons, give testimony of their personal faith in the Lord Jesus Christ and exhibit an understanding of what baptism means. It should be kept in mind that **the degree of one's faith is more important than the depth and the vastness of one's knowledge.** The mentally retarded person's knowledge may be quite limited, but his faith may be very strong.

The mentally retarded individual may be prepared for meeting with the pastor, deacon, and congregation by being encouraged to share his testimony in the worship service as well as by the content given in the Bible lesson time.

7. THE OFFERING. The mentally retarded need to be taught principles of Biblical giving and given the opportunity to share in God's work. The value or significance of money may not be known by some of the worshippers. Instruction should be given so that the retarded can understand how the offering is used (to heat the church building, for lights, books, etc.). Communication with parents, guardians, or group home managers or staff is most desirable so that there is no misunderstanding concerning why the students need to bring money. Offering envelopes may be helpful in preventing lost money or dropping coins on the floor. Ushers need to be trained in the procedures for taking the offering and participants need to be taught how to pass the offering plate. It may be meaningful to have a special project for which the offering will be used if the church policy allows.

8. PHYSICAL EXERCISE. The physical needs of the individuals should be considered in structuring the worship service. It may be necessary to change positions or to do a simple exercise.

9. ORDER OF WORSHIP. The size, mental age levels, and functional skills of the individuals must be reflected in the elements and order of the worship service. The order may be patterned after the regular worship services with the added necessary features.

10. HANDWORK AND REFRESHMENTS. These may also have a place in the self-contained class. The degree or extent to which these items are used may depend upon local preference, the length of the total program (including Sunday School), and the abilities and needs of the group. The expression or activity time should not be a program or time-filler, but should be integrated and related to the total program structure. Suggestions for arts and crafts and expression time may be found in chapter 19.

The worship service will be meaningful both to the leaders and the worshippers when there is careful and consistent planning that takes into consideration the needs and abilities of the worshippers.

Further suggestions may be found in *Leading the Mentally Retarded in Worship,* by Welborne and Williams (see bibliography).

12

INITIATING A PROGRAM IN THE CHRISTIAN SCHOOL

The development and growth of the Christian day school ministries of churches across the land has brought a growing awareness of the secular humanism that is present in the public school system. Many Christian and even non-Christian families have removed their children from the public schools and placed them in Christian day schools to combat the influence of humanism, among other ungodly influences, upon their children. These schools by and large have served the normal children of the families involved.

Today there is an ever-increasing awareness among churches and Christian educators that the philosophy of secular humanism is permeating the field of special education. This awareness has caused some to challenge the church through its Christian day school ministry to provide for the educational and social needs of the retarded with the same zeal and concern that is evident for the normal child. This type of ministry is not without its areas of concern in implementation and operation.

The philosophy of Christian school education has the Word of God as its foundation. The same Biblical principles that have stirred churches to action with Christian day schools for normal children must now stir them to action for the education of exceptional children. God's concern is the same for all children.

1. THE CHURCH'S RESPONSIBILITY. Those individuals interested in establishing a class for the mentally retarded in the Christian school will need

to formulate a proposal for such a class to present to the pastor. As the under-shepherd of the flock, he must sense the burden. The church as a whole must then be convinced of its responsibility in this area of training. The burden for this class will need to be presented along with a careful analysis of the need. The congregation will need to be challenged to incorporate this area of education into the total educational ministry of the church to ensure the success of such an undertaking. (See chapter 4 for additional helps.)

2. DEVELOPMENT OF AN ADEQUATE PROGRAM. Before a class is initiated, an adequate program needs to be developed. One of the best ways to begin a special education program is to observe and evaluate existing special education programs in other Christian schools. Consultation with Christians in the field of special education will assist in broadening the scope of understanding for the church congregation. Reports to the church body by those involved in observations and consultations will be of great benefit to the congregation in developing a suitable program.

One of the most effective methods of information gathering and program development for the congregation would be to hold a workshop or a series of workshops with Christian individuals in the field of special education. Workshops of this nature reach a larger segment of the congregation than is possible through visitations and consultations.

When the decision to begin a special education class has been finalized, the search for a teacher begins. This step should not occur until plans to begin a class have reached the place of finalization by the church congregation.

Shepherds College of Special Education is developing a listing of trained teachers and thus is an ideal source for recruitment. Christian colleges also would be good sources of potentially qualified teachers.

3. ADMINISTRATION. The special education class should never exist as a separate entity in relation to the established programs within the framework of the local Christian school. The program must be directly responsible to the school administrator to ensure the smooth operation and success of the program. The administrator will, in part, determine the success of the program in relation to discipline factors and encouragement of the teacher, and will act as a liaison between the home, church, school and community.

4. OBJECTIVES. The primary goal is to **provide a Christ-centered education for the mentally retarded student whose parents belong to the local church.** Thus, we have the concept of the whole family in the church. The objectives are broken down into four general categories to provide:

    a. Spiritually—training at the level where the student functions, salvation and growth in Christian principles (see Rom. 13; Rom. 12:1, 2).

    b. Personal care skills—so the retarded person can take care of himself, reflecting the truth found in 1 Corinthians 6:19.

   c. Emotional growth—to build the truth centered around God's Word in relation to his mind being controlled by God. The I AM concept: God created me; I am a worthwhile individual (Ps. 139:14–23).

   d. Academics (functional activities)—in communication, math, and other related skill areas. "We earn money to live on and support ourselves (Gen. 3:17–19). We say thank you to God and return a tithe and love gifts to God."

   e. Vocational readiness/citizenship—to respect the flag of the United States, government, rules, laws, and regulations. Provide work skills in preparation for living semi-independently (1 Thess. 4:11; 2 Thess. 3:10; Psalm 104:23; Rom. 13:1).

   f. Leisure time—train in specific sports, hobbies, games and special interests other than work—all based on a separated Biblical position (Rom. 12:1,2)

5. PROGRAM SCOPE. Those individuals who are responsible for planning the Christian school's special education program must decide who will be served in the class and how they will be served. These decisions will be dependent upon the needs of the individuals for whom the program is designed to reach and serve. Possible administrative arrangements are:

   a. A resource classroom designed to give specific subject and tutorial aid to slow learners and educable mentally retarded students who are mainstreamed in the regular program

   b. A self-contained class for educable mentally retarded individuals

   c. A self-contained class for trainable mentally retarded individuals

   d. A self-contained class for severely mentally retarded individuals

   e. b,c, and d with some integration into regular programs (such as physical education, lunch, music, home economics)

   f. Vocational training class for secondary level MR students:
      Independent and self-help skills
      Survival skills
      Vocational training
      Work stations and job training
      Functional academics

6. ELIGIBILITY. Consideration as to what constitutes enrollment in the special education class is essential.

   a. Formal Assessment—Diagnostic Tests

     (1) Standard IQ Test—prior to enrollment in the special class, an IQ test should be administered by a registered psychologist. The IQ test will indicate where the student functions in relation to

his academic functioning as compared to his peers. IQ levels: Mild-educable 69-55, Moderate-trainable 55-40, Severe 40-25.

(2) I.T.P.A. (Illinois Test of Psycholinguistic Abilities)—This diagnostic test, administered by a certified psychologist or speech pathologist or educational consultant, will aid the classroom teacher in preparation of materials to meet the individual learning style of the students. It is recommended as an additional resource tool for those students testing within the range of 55-69 on the intelligence test.

(3) Vineland Social Maturity Scale or AAMD Adaptive Behavior Scales—In addition to academic learning, an assessment of the student's functional level in relation to personal care and social and emotional maturity is essential. These will indicate an approximate functional level in these skills.

b. Informal Assessment—School Assessment

(1) Preplacement Evaluation (see Appendix D).
This educational instrument was designed to determine a guideline for placement of students in various classes. It is high enough to determine the highest functioning level of second grade and the lowest level of prekindergarten.

(2) Other Tests Administered by Classroom Teacher

(a) Peabody Picture Vocabulary (a receptive and expressive language test)

(b) PIAT—Peabody Individual Achievement Test (a stimulus-oriented test in all school subjects, no writing)

(c) WRAT—Wide Range Achievement Test (math, reading, and spelling) are also helpful to the teacher or administrator as diagnostic tools.

c. Emotional/Behavioral Problems
Some mentally retarded students will demonstrate an inability to control their emotional outbursts, handle their frustrations appropriately, and thus behave appropriately. This is due partly to their inability to reason out situations, partly to learned behavior patterns. The class is not primarily set up to handle students who have extreme emotional problems. However, one can expect a limited amount of immature behavior and problems in proportion to the students' mental age of functioning. The general limits should be established beforehand to avoid misunderstandings when a problem occurs.

d. Physical Problems
A required physical examination prior to enrollment in the class and each year thereafter is recommended. Students enrolled in class

should be ambulatory and capable of moving from place to place independently without the teacher's help, as for example those walking with braces/crutches or those having coordination problems. Students should be given an informal motor-physical education survey test to aid in planning of recreation and games (see Appendix E).

It is recommended that the student be toilet trained and capable of feeding himself prior to admission to the class (that is, a minimum 3½ to 4-year-old functional level).

Seizures—only those students whose seizures are under control should be permitted to enter the program or remain in class. Dismissal from class when seizures occur frequently during the day and until such time as they are under control is essential. If medication is to be administered by the teacher, a written note from the doctor indicating the time and the amount must be received before medication is dispensed. A student with uncontrolled seizures can require a teacher's full attention, thus negating her effectiveness in the classroom.

7. CLASSROOM
   a. Physical Properties
      (1) Size—large enough to have several locations to do various activities. Indoor activities in the winter will necessitate a room large enough to do some physical activity (e.g., if no gym is provided).
      (2) Atmosphere—cheerful, semibright colors, plants, pictures, book display, etc., to add atmosphere to the room. Avoid clutter or too much distracting material.
      (3) Restrooms—either in the classroom or close by. Early school days will necessitate a great deal of help from the teacher. A scheduled time in the morning and afternoon will keep students from leaving the room at all times. Prior to recess is an excellent time to send them because they won't waste time while in the bathroom. You may also wish to use older students in the school to help supervise during restroom time.
      (4) Storage cabinets
         (a) Built into wall if possible like a kitchen or secured to avoid tipping over
         (b) Some which can be locked with a key
         (c) Open shelves for games, books, record player, records, and miscellaneous equipment
         (d) Cubicles (students' storage) for shoes, take home papers,

mittens, etc. (These may be located outside the room where the clothes are hung.)

b. Composition of Students—The design of the class is heterogenous in nature even though the chronological ages are within a particular span. Students will function at different mental, emotional, spiritual, and academic levels within the framework of the class depending upon their level of functioning within the academic grouping of TMRs and EMRs. Recommended class size should not exceed fifteen.

Integration—depending upon the functional level, higher-functioning students may participate in other programs such as sports, field trips and lunch periods with regular students.

8. TEACHER. He must be born again and be in agreement with the Christian school's policies and practices. He must believe that the Lord has called him to the special task of teaching the retarded individual. It should not be considered a job but a service unto which the Lord has called (Col. 3:16, 17, 22–25). He must rely on the Lord for wisdom in dealing with problems and teaching individual students (James 1:5, 6).

Experience in kindergarten through third grades with regular students is recommended before teaching special education. This may be in the Sunday School, AWANA, DVBS, or a similar program. He must be able to teach without becoming discouraged by the fact that he may not see success from day to day or year to year.

He must be a well-organized person, yet flexible enough to meet the changes when they occur. He should not tire of routine or need change often. He should have a real love for children at the nursery/beginner/primary age and be able to work with students who will remain at this level of functioning even though chronologically they are thirteen or fourteen.

He must be creative and able to teach concepts without having a program and prescribed curriculum. Kits and programmed learning materials will only be a source of reference for him.

9. COST. The salary of the teacher and the initial purchase of equipment and supplies will determine the financial base for the program. In addition to tuition, parents may also contribute items for the training skills in home economics such as eggs, flour, and staples, which the school would not usually consider as part of a budget. Individuals may support the special education program by direct support or provide scholarships. The local school policy should be followed. The special education teacher should be compensated equally with other teachers.

10. EQUIPMENT
   a. Furniture
      (1) Adjustable desks and chairs

    (2) Teacher's desk and chair

    (3) Adjustable table and chairs for small group work (kidney-shaped if funds are available)

    (4) Filing cabinet

 b. Teaching Aids

    (1) Record player/tape recorder-one unit if possible

    (2) Magnetic chalkboard

    (3) Painting Easel

    (4) Sand Table

 c. General Supplies

Same as regular school—will need more of them because of the amount of work required to accomplish one task. Primary pencils, training scissors (*a must*), regular scissors, painting smocks, primary paper (1″ ruled) or transition paper, paste, finger paint, paint, 1″ paint brushes, ½″ paint brushes, construction paper, primary size crayons

 d. Textbooks and Auxiliary Items

    (1) Regular program—Usually you will use the same books as in a regular program, depending upon the mental age of the student. You will need a wide range of textbooks in reading, math, speech, (language), and social studies.

    (2) Central Supply—If your school has a central supply for textbooks, have the principal order a few extra books to use in your department with a teacher's edition.

    (3) Reading textbooks—will probably be geared to sight words rather than phonetic approach to reading.

    (4) Speech (Language Kits)—Peabody Kit is recommended but you may also choose from other widely known programs. Listening records and tapes are desirable for your own class.

    (5) Auxiliary items—flash cards, games, charts, ditto materials, counting aids, etc.

 e. Home Economics

A kitchen, stove and refrigerator are essential for the program. The class should be permitted to use the kitchen area of the church or school or have its own kitchen. Simple skills such as cooking a meal, baking cakes and cookies, and opening soup should be taught. Use the basic eight food groups for simple meal preparation.

 f. Vocational Readiness

Vocational readiness skills such as sorting, folding, color matching, classroom chores, and timed manual tasks should be taught from the very beginning of the child's formal training. These skills should be expanded and new skills added as the child develops and advances through school.

11. INDIVIDUALIZING INSTRUCTION. In view of the varying functional levels of the students within the class, developing individual or small group plans will likely be the most effective method of teaching the class. Individual abilities and needs should be taken into account when developing a student's plan. This method of planning and teaching requires a great deal of time and effort on the part of the teacher but results of this method should prove the most productive for the students involved. (See Appendix F. This planning outline may serve as a guide to individualized planning. Adaptations and variations of such a guide will be determined by the various levels and circumstances of the school using it.)

12. TECHNICAL ASSISTANCE. Staff members of Shepherds, Inc., in Union Grove, Wisconsin, are available for workshops and consultation. In addition to this, curriculum guidelines are being developed by Shepherds' staff to aid in the implementation of classes as Christian schools develop plans for special education classes in their schools.

13

EXPANDING TO OTHER PROGRAMS

G uidelines have been shared concerning the launching of the three major areas of a local church's ministry to the mentally retarded, namely **Sunday School, worship** and the **Christian day school**. This does not imply that these three are more important than other possible ministries. Local priority may determine another ministry to be more important. The principles and guidelines already considered also serve as general guidelines in expanding to these other ministry options that are available to the local church. This chapter and the next will not give the detailed guides as was given for the basic three ministries but will define the role and importance of the optional ministry as well as give important facts to be considered.

Any one of these additional ministries could be evaluated as a priority by a local church. Some of these may be launched at the same time as other ministries.

Prayer Meeting

The mentally retarded need to be taught what prayer is, the importance of prayer and how to pray. Instruction is also needed in the areas of praying individually and in a group. The retarded individual will develop his ability to pray by experience in praying. The prayer meeting may therefore become very meaningful to the retarded. For most of the retarded, a separate prayer meeting is preferred. After readiness preparation, high functioning adults may participate in the regular prayer meeting service. Retarded children may participate in the regular children's prayer meeting if such is conducted by the local church. Principles for teaching prayer are found in chapter 18.

Daily Vacation Bible School

A church which has established Sunday School programming could easily expand its programming to include a DVBS program. Daily Vacation Bible School may also be the initial program used by a church to launch its special education program for the retarded. In planning a DVBS program, consideration should be given to the attention span and physical limitations of the retarded. DVBS also gives an opportunity to minister to the needs of others in the community who do not participate in the church's ministries. Parents may welcome the morning off for one or two weeks. Shephderds, Inc., has a DVBS curriculum.

Home Bible Classes/Individual and Group Discipling

These may be an effective means of teaching the mentally retarded who reside in group homes, nursing homes, training schools or institutions in the church's community. Many of the retarded may not attend the ministries for the retarded in the local church. What about a Bible class for one? This is the emphasis of the individual discipling ministry that is a part of the ministry of the local church. This could also be done in the case of a mentally retarded individual. Joni Eareckson wrote of the importance of a 16-year-old friend who came into her life as her Bible teacher when she really needed help (*A Step Further*, p. 47).

Youth/Club Programs

A program emphasis for the mentally retarded may be structured as part of the church's youth ministry or weekday club ministry. Churches using the AWANA Youth Association (3201 Tollview Drive, Rolling Meadows, Illinois 60008) program should consider adding the AWANA Friends Club for the mentally retarded.

Adopted Grandparents Program

This program offers the opportunity for adult Christians to minister to the needs of the retarded by taking a personal interest in them. It is not feasible to list all the practical areas that are being explored. In some cases, the program is called Aunts and Uncles, or similar names. The idea is to take on care of a retarded person and do things with him such as attending church, attending sporting events, a trip to the adopters' home, going out to eat, field trips, shopping and swimming, as well as giving special emphasis on holidays, birthdays, and other special occasions. The adopters may sponsor them at camps, banquets, etc. In some areas, the adopters spend time in working with the retarded in their educational and training programs.

Respite Ministry

A family often does not escape the hassle of the twenty-four hour care of their child or adult. In this program, someone else cares for the retarded person so that the parents and family can do some of the things they would really like to do. Relief from responsibilities for a part of a day, a full day, an evening, or even a week can be very beneficial to the parents and family members. It may even involve providing child/adult care or babysitting so that the parents can attend church services, go to church conferences or socials, or attend to family business. Many parents have expressed the need for help in this area but, with sadness, relate that no one ever offered.

Social and Recreational Ministries

Many retarded tend to be isolated socially because of their handicaps and are limited in recreation because of their physical condition and reasoning ability. A program designed specifically in light of their needs and abilities can help them to have more to do than sitting before a TV set. Sunday School classes and youth groups can effectively plan outings for the retarded or take them along with them (i.e., fishing, to the beach, picnic with games, etc.). Some churches have retarded on their church-sponsored softball or basketball teams and see that they go to games to cheer for their favorite players as well (see chapter 22).

Camping

Camping is one special means of social and recreational programming. It could include regular summer camp, church day camping, and two to three day camping retreats. (A much anticipated and enjoyable program for residents of Shepherds has been the regular yearly camping experiences at the state GARBC camp.) In the secular world, the National Association for Retarded Citizens has been sponsoring camps for the retarded for a long time. Shepherds can put you in touch with Christian special education camp ministries.

Group Homes and Sheltered Workshops

Current programming for the mentally retarded emphasizes returning the retarded to their homes and local communities to live and to work.

In a *Group Home,* a group of unrelated residents live in a residential neighborhood with supervision and support from resident or live-in group home managers or counselors. Generally, smaller group homes would house eight or less in normal residential size homes. Larger group homes would house eight or more residents in larger duplex or apartment size homes in or near residential areas.

Many group home residents are not able to function in the competitive job world. These residents would go to a *sheltered workshop* during normal work hours where they would receive vocational and work evaluation, and work training and experience. Acceptable work habits and job skills would also be developed. The workshop would provide jobs for those who cannot work in the community and place qualified residents in community jobs.

These programs would allow the Biblical priorities of the church to be carried out in the living and working situations of the retarded. Such specialty programs could be conducted and sponsored by a local church or a group of local churches in a large metropolitan area. Shepherds, Inc., can assist you in setting up these programs.

Because group homes and sheltered workshops normally require some type of governmental approval, churches planning such programs should check out applicable regulations before beginning.

There is a variety of ministry options available to the local church that has a desire to meet the needs of the mentally retarded. Local needs and priorities will help the church to decide what to include and how to proceed. The suggestion is to start somewhere and then expand as the need arises.

Section Four

PRINCIPLES OF WORKING WITH THE MENTALLY RETARDED

All the thinking, planning, preparation and training culminate in the day that the actual ministry begins in a local church. At this time, the need for practical helps is easily recognized. What? and How? become very important questions.

This section considers a number of practical helps and methods areas that a local church special education staff should consider.

"For precept must be upon precept,
. . . line upon line,
. . . here a little, and there a little" (Isa. 28:10).

"The law of the LORD is perfect,
converting the soul:
the testimony of the LORD is sure,
making wise the simple" (Ps. 19:7).

14

Curriculum Planning and Development

What mental picture does the word *curriculum* convey to you?

Tim was in a regular third grade class in a consolidated school system. He was active in his AWANA program and had earned enough points to go to a roller skating party with his group. Wednesday morning, he was all excited and bubbling when he arrived at school. "Miss Glanville, I'm going to a roller skating party on Saturday in AWANA, but I don't even know what roller skates are!"

Tim's English curriculum for that day was to use the Sears catalog to locate a picture of roller skates as well as the encyclopedia to aid in concept formation.

At this point in your reading, I can hear you say, "But what will the principal say? Tim isn't doing the same English as the rest of the class! How does he receive a grade for his work?" To answer your questions, our philosophy regarding curriculum is that it must be *pupil centered* rather than book administered. The curriculum merely serves as a road map to verify the main route to travel. It does not express the numerous minute paths to take in order to arrive at your destination. For example, locate various passages of Scripture where Jesus is interacting either with an individual or group of people. Write down the central theme (thought, idea, types of sentences) and this concept may be considered as the curriculum. Did you notice that in most of the teaching/learning interaction, Jesus utilized the facts, opinions, attitudes, values, questions, and particular circumstances of the audience, as well as individuals, to meet the represented needs of the learner?

Jesus was pupil-centered in the teaching/learning process. Luke 6:40, "The disciple [pupil] is not above his master: but every one that is perfect shall be as his master" (brackets are author's).

The Student

In knowing your pupils, the availability for understanding them is found in the Word of God. Hebrews 4:16 (Amplified New Testament), "Let us then fearlessly and confidently and boldly draw near to the throne of grace—the throne of God's unmerited favor [to us sinners]: that we may receive mercy [for our failures] and find grace to help in good time for every need—appropriate help and well-timed help, coming just when you need it."

The mentally retarded individual is a person first, then he is mentally retarded. He has the same basic requirements for good mental health, such as love, success, pain, frustration, fear and joy, as normal people. Coupled with these basic factors is the classification system known as mental retardation. This system classifies groups of students that are homogenous according to IQ, yet very heterogenous in nature. Individual students will have different likes such as favorite food or color, dislikes such as baseball or football, physical needs and learning styles. These factors will require additional interaction of the teacher with the student in his living environment either as he resides with his family or in a residential facility in the community.

Once these individual assessments are determined, they are then woven into the outlined materials in the curriculum.

The reader should also keep in mind that the writer of the curriculum may have a different sampling of population as well as background in working with exceptionalities. Therefore, all materials that are introduced are required to form a curriculum intersect with all areas of the pupils' learning environment.

The teacher and writer depend upon the Holy Spirit in the planning of the lesson. The teacher considers the learners' needs and adjusts this to the curriculum as he depends upon the Holy Spirit in the presentation of the lesson.

The Lesson

"Never underestimate the power of the Holy Spirit to illuminate the heart of your students." Three areas presented in the Sunday School lesson are:

Cognitive
Knowledge, facts learned

Affective
Feelings, attitudes

Behavioral
Application of the lesson

One kindergarten girl was overheard saying, "I pledge to the Christmas flag" (I pledge allegiance to the Christian flag.) This girl was operating at the first level of learning—the awareness level. She had quoted all the words—she had the factual knowledge—but she did not have the ability to make judgments to see if she could hear the words the same as her peers. She did, however, watch and pledge to the correct flag.

The Cognitive level, in the lesson presentation to the mentally retarded, in the teaching/learning process refers to factual information or the facts to be learned by the student. How many helpers (disciples) did Jesus have? Where was Jesus born? What day do you go to church? What is this symbol?, etc.

The majority of Trainable Mentally Retarded students with IQs of 25-54 operate within this level in a lesson presentation. They are able to learn (memorize) factual information and after consistent repetition retain the knowledge and recite it back to the teacher. This type of teaching/learning is demonstrated in catechism classes.

The second level of lesson presentation is the Affective Domain, which pertains to the student's feelings and attitudes. On this plane, the retarded student not only is aware of the concepts as they have been presented but has also memorized some basic facts and has made simple judgments and inferences. This level may also include the student's sensitivity to his own needs as well as to the needs of others in his environment.

For example, the student can be taught to respond to Miss Kouf, who is sad because her mother died. He can identify with how Jesus felt when a boy was sick. You can show him from a picture that a boy is happy— he is smiling. As noted, the Affective Domain is a very basic low functional level with some of the feelings being memorized while others are spontaneous in nature.

The final level to measure in the lesson is the most difficult to achieve and is known as the Behavioral (application) stage. Since TMR and most EMR students function within the framework of concrete thinkers, they are unable to translate lessons learned from one situation to another or make practical application. Situations in life cannot always be taught ahead of time, so they must rely partially on others in the decision-making process. This level develops as the student progresses in the teaching/learning process, but at the mature level, the TMR student may be operating at the level of a 3- to 5-year-old child chronologically.

For example, Dr. Wood frequently reminds Shepherds staff members of a particular resident and his faith. While teaching the concept, ". . .come before His presence with singing" (Ps. 100:2), the teacher told the students it was like coming when their names were called. She called several students, then a young man's name. He jumped out of his chair, ran to her and threw his arms around her. What did she do? Nothing! When asked why he did it, the child said, "When Jesus says 'Come,' He means 'Come!' "

Method-Technique

In order to be an effective teacher with the mentally retarded individual, the teacher should be familiar with the modality pathway by which the student learns. No curriculum ideas will be profitable to the teacher unless this essential concept is determined prior to the introduction of the lesson.

What is modality learning? It is the particular method(s) by which the mentally retarded individual incorporates the senses of seeing, hearing, tasting, smelling and touching into the process of learning. This knowledge must be understood and applied by the student from previous lessons (past), the new material (present), and the future weeks of lessons. When the student is able to make judgments, compare/contrast ideas, and think in abstract situations, it is commonly referred to as *conceptual thinking* (behavioral level). For example: What is stealing? One boy in the class was able to name several things such as taking chalk, taking colors from another student's desk, and taking cookies out of the cookie jar "when no one was looking." He also could identify pictures of someone stealing money, shoplifting, etc. However, he frequently had the teacher's magic marker in his pocket! After several years of Bible lessons, he was able to make the application that taking anything that didn't belong to him was stealing and was sin.

Visual refers to instruction through the sense of sight. Some TMR students are able to learn to read printed symbols (vocabulary words) and to translate them into corresponding word meanings (functional definition of the printed letters/symbols). For example: Reading printed symbols: Mary, Joseph, Bible, Jesus, church, etc. After they have mastered this process, the student is able to memorize and retain this information for future learning. These students usually function at the higher level of the IQ range for the TMR.

Learning in school, in AWANA and in church is rewarding as the retarded have mastered, at their functional level, the ability to use a skill for future independence and learning. Their word recognition, generally speaking, is about two years above their ability to give the corresponding meanings. The average TMR student, although capable of reading words and understanding their meanings, lacks the conceptual skill for reading to obtain information from the printed page. Therefore they are referred to as word readers (that is, they lack comprehension skills to accompany their high vocabulary of sight words).

Auditory refers to instruction through the sense of hearing. The TMR and EMR who is unable to learn through the visual method alone may be able to process (learn) information through the two senses. In this way, he may be introduced to a visual and auditory clue for instructional purposes. For example: 1 + 1 = 2. He repeats this concept but he also has the visual counterpart to assist him. The problem in learning is manifested when he is unable to rid himself of the oral reinforcement. When he sees the combination 1 + 1 = and is asked for the answer, he is unable to visualize the symbol to go with the corresponding auditory response. If a student is unable to do this, it is necessary to teach him through the auditory method. This is primarily the recite, hear, say procedure. The student totally depends upon the teacher for his basic instructional needs. Learning, therefore, is dependent upon oral recitation and constant review. The use of flannelgraph, show 'n tell, object lessons, and other visuals while telling the story helps the student learn. See chapters 15-19 for teaching helps in other curricular areas.

If the student has the ability to retain information through the auditory pathway, he may be able to function semi-independently in society and retain a position in a sheltered workshop.

Kinesthetic refers to the movement of limbs using muscles to accomplish the task. For example: see, recite and trace in the air. Spelling words, math combination, etc., may be taught with the see, say, trace method. Most students will not use this step but will profit from tactile modality.

Tactile refers to any tangible object that may be traced or touched. This modality is an individualized approach to teaching and is the longest technique administered to teach the retarded student. The teacher must print or write every selection of material so the student can trace it or feel it. Sandpaper, cotton, wax, string, and glue are possible tactile surfaces that may be used. After the student has mastered the concept through the tactile approach, he is then able to make the transferences to the visual method if he is able to retain what he has learned. In the Sunday School program, touch and feel books (such as Creation—feeling the grass, sand, textures) may be used with various lessons.

Taste and smell are also included in the modality method of learning but are considered as minor elements. You may use these, however, in selected lessons.

To be an effective teacher with the mentally retarded using curricula that have been developed or in the preparation of your own, remember to do the following:

C arefully select the aim/goal for each lesson.

U nderstand and apply the modalities by which your students learn.

R epeat constantly.

R emember to pray for your students as well as the lesson content.

I ntegrate Biblical truths familiar to the student as well as examples from their lives.

C urriculum—use it as a basic guide and adapt it to the needs of your particular students.

U tilize various teaching techniques to reinforce learning.

L ean upon the Holy Spirit to teach you and to reach the MR for Christ.

U se pupil-centered material.

M otivate the students to learn through his interests.

Remember that when you are tired of teaching the concept, the mentally retarded individual has just begun to learn.

"Those things, which ye have both learned and received,
and heard, and seen in me, do:
and the God of peace shall be with you" (Phil. 4:9).

V.A.K.T.O.G					
Total Modality System					
V	A	K	T	*O	*G
I	U	I	A	L	U
S	D	N	C	F	S
U	I	E	T	A	T
A	T	S	I	C	O
L	O	T	L	T	R
	R	H	E	O	I
	Y	E		R	A
		T		Y	L
		I			
		C			

MR students learn basic skills
through one primary modality or
a combination of modalities.

*Taste and smell are also included in the multi-sensory system but are considered as minor elements. You may, however, use them in selected lessons in your curriculum.

15

GENERAL TEACHING PRINCIPLES

I t is important to keep in mind that the mentally retarded have the same basic needs for love, understanding, acceptance, and success as normal children. The attitude of those who work with them is crucial because the retarded quickly discern whether they are accepted for who they are and how you feel concerning them. It has been said that it takes common sense and basic teaching skills to work with the retarded.

Each person is uniquely created by God with some of the similar characteristics of the mentally retarded. It is important to know where the retarded individual is presently functioning so that realistic expectations may be developed in light of his strengths and weaknesses. The following charts will help you to determine the teaching techniques to use. Remember that "success builds success."

Attention Difficulties:	1. Schedule shorter work periods (5-20 minutes depending upon the interest and aptitude of the group members). Begin with short periods and progress to longer ones.
	2. Arrange materials, etc., with proper attention cues to captivate interest and attention.
	3. Eliminate distracting and irrelevant stimuli (pull shades, turn off music, use study cubicles). An uncluttered room is essential in working with the retarded. Be sure your own dress does not distract (i.e., stay away from too much pattern in clothing.)

4. Tasks should be simple, brief, sequential, and lead to successful achievement.
5. Alternate segments of quiet listening and active physical participation. Watch for signs of fatigue or distress.
6. Give clear and precise instructions as to what is expected. Do not allow inattention to continue.
7. Insist that a task be completed by consistently returning to the task at hand with additional help or encouragement.

Active/Hyperactive:
1. Plan sessions to include short sections with movement in between.
2. Include movement and exercise in your sessions.
3. Be ready and prepared for the unexpected.
4. Set times when they must sit on the chair and be quiet—for prayer, etc.

Concrete/Literal Thinker:
1. Present one concept at a time.
2. Emphasize literal, real and meaningful materials and content.
3. Relate new concepts and ideas to something that is already known.
4. Time and distance facts or references must be carefully explained and illustrated.
5. If analogies are used, present in terms of real or concrete explanation and illustrations.
6. Use multisensory approaches to learning. (See Curriculum Planning/chapter 14)
7. Mean what you say and say what you mean.
8. Plan to include first hand experience with real objects and situations, as well as pictures, slides, films of real objects.
9. Break down areas into small sections and arrange in sequence.

Memory Deficits:
1. Make requests or commands short, simple, using vocabulary at mental age, and related to the task desired.
2. Plan for much repetition and review until the material is learned. Review over various periods of time, i.e., hourly, daily, weekly.
3. Divide material to be learned into smaller sec-

tions and learn one at a time. Go back over these sections and repeat when learning the new material (i.e., a new section). Teach each four to six weeks using different learning and teaching methods. Repetition is vital!

4. Provide a variety of memorizing methods to aid in learning, i.e., visualization, singing, games, breaking down into small parts, etc.

5. If possible, appeal to all six of the sensory areas (vision, hearing, feeling, motion, smell, taste) to facilitate learning.

6. Present material so that progression is made from the easy to the more difficult.

7. Avoid the pressure of planning to do more than you have time for by reorganizing your lesson plans.

Generalization Deficits:

1. Show how the knowledge area to be learned would appear in different situations in the child's experience.

2. Present the concept in a variety of ways of relationships.

3. Provide help in transferring knowledge from situation to situation.

Lack of Motivation

1. Show enthusiasm and personal interest as a teacher or worker.

2. Use a variety of presentation methods and length of units or sessions.

3. Reward small achievement or success.

4. Use progress and reward charts to show where the student is going and how much he has achieved.

5. Incorporate a variety of incentives into all learning situations.

6. Give the feeling of success or achievement by breaking tasks down into various component steps that can be accomplished one at a time.

7. Continue to present challenges that are within the realm of the child's abilities.

8. Give lots of recognition and praise and don't be insincere or patronizing.

9. Outline carefully what is expected and how to arrive at the desired goal.
10. Use Interest Centers.

Low Self Esteem/ Concept:

1. Demonstrate and encourage an attitude of acceptance for each child.
2. Spend time talking with each one about the things of interest to him.
3. Involve the student in doing things in the areas of his strength and interests.
4. Break down tasks into smallest components so that he can experience success instead of failure.
5. Provide feedback so that the student knows that he has responded correctly.
6. Practice and review so that the student develops confidence in completion of tasks.
7. Spend time with the student in his home and in outside activities.
8. Be ready to give assistance to a student who is becoming frustrated.

Self-Centered:

1. Encourage group participation with sharing and recognition of others who achieve.
2. Do not allow the student to control the situation, dominate others, or insist on his own way.
3. If temper tantrums exist, remind him that he still has to complete the task.
4. Use generous amounts of praise for appropriate attitudes and behavior, i.e., sharing, thoughtfulness.

Desire for Routine:

1. Establish a regular structure or routine.
2. Plan and prepare for necessary changes whenever possible.
3. Develop a sequence for proceeding from one thing to another.
4. Use that which is familiar or known as a bridge to introduce the new materials or programs.

Language Deficits:

1. Use simple and precise vocabulary.
2. Explain new words/concepts carefully.
3. Plan for alternative means of expressive language (communication boards, gestures, etc.)

4. Encourage correct speech/language use.

Social Deficits: 1. Emphasize and practice basic social living skills, i.e., manners, etiquette, grooming, hygiene, dress.

2. Establish and practice the importance of living according to the rules of God's Word, church, AWANA club, home, school, and society.

3. Reinforce the desired skills and eliminate the nondesirable behaviors.

4. Incorporate variety of independent living skills wherever possible.

16

MINISTERING THROUGH INTEREST CENTERS

An interest center is a special section of a classroom designated for minireview, independent achievement and the introduction of new Biblical concepts. It may be designed for those individuals who arrive early and have nothing to do before the class session begins or as part of the actual teaching lesson for that day. This will depend upon the population to whom you minister in your individual community. However, if you bus your students, this center is necessary as it will help quiet the students and prepare them for the actual class or worship time.

Suggested ideas for interest centers:
1. Models such as Bible homes
2. Pictures to circle . . . things I am afraid of, how God takes care of me, etc.
3. Individualized puzzles made from old Sunday School pictures
4. Review games
5. Prerecorded cassette tapes—songs and stories
6. Pictures backed with flannel to put in correct sequences or captions
7. Pieces of scrap material to dress like Joseph, Mary, etc.

Why should you use interest centers as part of your teaching time?

FIRST: Interest centers capture the attention of your students when they arrive in your room. You may begin to teach Bible concepts before the entire group arrives. Thus, it provides individual attention for those quiet students or, better still, for those active talkative ones.

SECOND: Interest centers provide individual time to "know your students." It's exciting to the student to tell his teacher about grandma coming to visit, his first paycheck, his new shirt, or about what happened at school or work. During the interest center time, you can find out many things about the happenings of the week that can be related to your lesson. **The best illustrations you use in your teaching time are those centered around the lives of the students you teach.**

THIRD: Interest centers provide factual information concerning the concepts of the lessons in a visualized manner. In one Bible class, when asked, "What do cows eat?", all types of answers were given—"sandwiches, milk, cake." The Bible teacher brought grass and hay to the classroom so the students could see and feel it. Then they understood why the choices of Abraham and Lot were important.

FOURTH: Interest centers provide review concerning the concepts taught. For instance, why did Lot want to fight with Abraham? "Because he wanted all the grass land." Was this the best choice? "No, Lot didn't know what God was going to do." These concepts may be integrated throughout all the sessions as they relate to individual lessons that build toward the Series Aim.

FIFTH: Interest centers also provide handwork activities. Students enjoy handwork activities they can take home and use to recreate the teaching lesson. As they tell the story to their families, it serves as an extension of the teaching session as well as providing repetition.

SIXTH: Interest centers provide a multisensory approach to teaching. Pictures, puzzles, diagrams, role playing, films and show 'n tell reflect the entire teaching/learning situation. If you haven't used interest centers before, try them! They are a vital part of the teaching/learning process.

17

MINISTERING THROUGH MUSIC

Music has been described as the universal language of the soul—a description that is emphasized in ministering to the needs of the mentally retarded. Music is an effective teaching tool as well as a means of personal joy and satisfaction. Because the retarded like to sing or listen to music, music may reach them when other methods fail. For some, it may be their first means of cummunication. Moreover, it is not necessary to read in order to sing and enjoy music. Even the most severely retarded find joy and satisfaction in music.

Music is also a vital part of religious education and worship. The Scriptures abound with references to music. In Psalm 100, we are instructed to "Make a joyful noise unto the Lord" and to "Come before His presence with singing." Psalm 95:1 states that we are to "Sing unto the Lord" and to "Make a joyful noise." In Ephesians 5:19, the evidence of the control of the Holy Spirit is given as "Speaking to yourselves in psalms, hymns, and spiritual songs, singing and making melody in your heart to the Lord." Colossians 3:16 adds the idea of "singing with grace in our hearts" when we let the "Word of Christ dwell in us." These areas are important to the retarded.

Importance of Music

From a study of various music publications, it is possible to compile a long list of reasons why music is important in meeting the needs of the mentally retarded. The following seem to be significant:

1. Music has an important place in Biblical worship and education. Bib-

lical truth can be taught and reinforced through music. Music enhances and facilitates worship by creating an atmosphere for worship and creating a desire to participate.

2. Singing and music are expressive experiences. Through vocal and physical means, the retarded can express emotions, moods, and ideas that they would or could not do through other means. For some, the physical and emotional release is important.

3. Music helps to develop a person's well-being and self-worth through enjoyment and relaxation.

4. Music motivates the learner, enriches experiences, and unifies a group in a unique way (Monroe, 1980).

5. As an educational tool, music is used to teach academics and Biblical truth, develop social skills, introduce stories or instructional units, impart new skills, demonstrate abilities or concepts, supplement games and memory work and to emphasize holidays and special days.

6. Music enhances social development through group participation, sharing, following directions, and taking turns.

7. Music aids in developing learning, stimulating recall and developing auditory and vocal discrimination.

Types of Musical Emphasis

The scope of the music program will be dependent upon the needs and abilities of the individual and of the group, as well as the skill of the teachers, etc. The music emphasis may include:

1. Listening to music, including the mechanics of selecting and using records and tapes, for entertainment, learning and leisure enjoyment

2. Music education—instruction in the mechanics of music, reading music, singing, rhythm instruments and playing an instrument

3. Music therapy—using music to improve gross and fine motor skills, encourage cooperation and participation and increase the ability to follow directions

4. Exercising to music and musical games

5. Using music for academic and Biblical instruction

6. Participation in choirs, solos and rhythm bands

7. Dramatic presentations of what the music says or how it is felt

8. Music appreciation

Tips for Music Selection

1. Use music in every activity with the retarded.

2. Select songs for their direct value in teaching Biblical truth because the message is important.

3. Music should be related to the total program and not just a time consumer or filler.

4. Select music in light of the group's level of learning and understanding, interest level and attention span.

5. The melody should be simple, of moderate length and have an easy vocal range.

6. Songs selected should bring pleasure and enjoyment to the individuals.

7. The words should have meaning and be related to the personal life of the group.

8. Avoid fast, syncopated, or tongue-twister type music. This includes much contemporary "Christian" music.

9. Select songs with words that are easy to pronounce.

10. Teach new songs sparingly—familiar songs facilitate understanding and enjoyment as they are repeated. Introduce new songs after the previous songs have been thoroughly learned.

11. Provide for a variety of musical experiences.

12. Use songs with repetitive word or music components that will aid in learning them.

13. Use a variety of methods in teaching songs.

14. When you ask for favorites, give them a selection of songs from which to choose.

15. Avoid songs with symbolic or hidden meaning.

16. Use a variety of types of songs (hymns, choruses, fun choruses, action songs, musical game songs, ageless songs, holiday songs, self-composed songs).

17. Correlate the songs with the theme, Bible lesson, memory work, application, etc.

Teaching Songs

A person does not have to be a proficient musician to use music effectively. An important key is to know the song first before attempting to teach it to others. The teacher may have to use someone else to assist her with the music or to have the musical part of the program on tape. Instruction should also be given on how to learn the song and how to sing. Some general principles are:

1. Introduce the song by using pictures, illustrations, objects, Bible verses.
2. Sing and play the entire song through one or more times.
3. Read the words and sound out difficult words carefully and slowly.
4. Explain the meaning of the words, phrases, verse and entire song.
5. Interpret the changes in pitch, mood or volume.
6. Teach the song word by word, phrase by phrase or line by line.
7. Practice: repeat, repeat, repeat!
8. Use visualized songs to present words and ideas.
9. Make sure they are singing the words correctly.
10. Be enthusiastic and joyful.
11. Repeat songs on a regular basis, such as from day to day, until they are thoroughly learned.
12. Tape the music to be used. The initial presentation can thus be slower so that both words and melody may be followed. Leave adequate space between songs when using several selections.

Teaching Methods

A. *Visual*

1. Blackboard
2. Flannelgraph
3. Pictures
4. Music Wheel
5. Books (prepared)
6. Sign Language
7. Rebus
8. Flash Cards
9. Posters
10. Bulletin Boards
11. Drama
12. Visualized Songs
13. Overhead Projector
14. Games
15. Puppets

B. *Auditory*

1. Instruments
2. Tape Recorder
3. Record Player
4. Soloist

C. *Tactile*

1. Actions
2. Marching/other movement
3. Drama
4. Sign Language
5. Vibrations of piano
6. Holding visual songs
7. Objects—clothes pins, 10 little Indians
8. Tapping, Clapping
9. Games

Mentally Retarded learn by:
1. Rote
2. Imitation
3. Repetition

For high functioning, seeing the music may help them to associate note movement and value. They can see how soon a word is sung so that they can "keep together" during a song.

Twenty-Two Ways to Teach a Song by JoAnn Butler (Choristers Guild, P.O. Box 38188, Dallas, TX 75238) gives a variety of specific helps in different ways to teach a song.

Although the goals, methods and musical selections may vary depending upon the needs and interests of the individuals and group, music is an effective tool to meet the needs of the mentally retarded. Thus, music will have a prominent place in any ministry to the mentally retarded.

18

PRAYER AND
SCRIPTURE MEMORIZATION

Prayer

Prayer is as vital in the lives of the mentally retarded as it is for normal individuals. They need to learn and feel that talking to God in prayer is a natural part of the life of those who love Him. Prayer should also be an effective part of praise and worship.

As individuals, the mentally retarded need to develop the practice of bringing their true feelings and concerns directly to God. In addition, they can learn to pray in small or large groups as well as learn how to listen while others are praying.

In ministering to the mentally retarded, leaders or teachers should prepare the individuals by presenting the Biblical concepts concerning prayer and assisting them in developing a prayer life through daily practice.

The following outline is effective in preparing the mentally retarded for prayer.

    A. *What is prayer?*
        1. Prayer is talking to God.
        2. God is alive and in Heaven.
        3. God is Holy and all powerful.
        4. We pray to God—not to idols.
    B. *Who can pray?*
        1. We must be saved in order for God to hear and answer our prayer.
        2. God hears the prayer of faith for salvation.

3. God does not hear us if we have sin in our lives.
4. We should confess our sins to God.
5. God wants to answer our prayer.

*The complete lesson series is available from Shepherds, Inc., under the title of *PRAYER*.

    C. *What is the pattern for prayer?*
       1. Call God by His name—our Father
       2. Confess our sin—we are sorry for our sin
       3. Saying thank You to God
       4. Asking for help and the things we need
       5. Praying in Jesus' name
       6. Concluding our prayer
    D. *How do we pray?*
       1. Praying in Jesus Name
       2. Praying with bowed head and closed eyes
       3. Praying for God's will to be done
       4. Praying in faith believing
    E. *When, Why, Where should we pray?*
       1. Morning
       2. Evening
       3. Specific occasions—parties, etc.
       4. For food, health, families
       5. In church, at home, meal table, bedroom
    F. *How Does God answer prayer?*
       1. God does not always give us what we want.
       2. We can pray for wrong things.
       3. God always knows best.
       4. God can answer yes, no, wait.

General Concepts

1. Explain to students that we should be quiet during prayer. One person talks to God while all the others are polite by listening and not doing other things.

2. Explain that we close our eyes to keep us thinking about God. We are not seeing other things or looking at what our friends may be doing.

3. Explain that we fold our hands to keep from playing with things or touching other people. (Older teens or adults may be taught to fold their arms or place their hands on their legs.)

4. Have each person pray immediately after the request so that he won't forget his request.

5. As they mature through experience, give out more than one request.

6. In presession training sessions, ask whether they want to pray.

7. When they are learning to pray, have them repeat after you, short prayers that express their desire, need or a particular request.

8. Use prayer cards with pictures to help them remember a particular request.

9. If they tend to mumble on, aid them by whispering "Amen" as they may need to be reminded how to conclude their prayer.

10. Use a variety of prayer methods.
   a. Request time
   b. Thanksgiving time
   c. Pray for specific needs.
   d. Use a prayer family visual aid, using your hand with a request for each finger.

Remember that the interest and level of achievement will be dependent upon individuals. Practice is important to learning.

Scripture Memorization

Thy word have I hid in mine heart,
that I might not sin against thee (Ps. 119:11).

Learning and understanding the Scriptures and applying them in daily living practices are vital and Biblical norms for anyone. For the most part, memorization may be difficult for the retarded because of short term memory deficits and inability to understand or comprehend the meaning or significance. Repetition of the memory verse and its use in a variety of ways are thus very important.

The memory verse or verses should be selected in view of the daily living needs of the retarded, and should be within their understanding capabilities. These verses should be correlated with their Sunday School lessons or worship service materials. We should not underestimate their Scripture learning ability as many have memorized large passages of Scripture as well as many Scripture-related gospel songs and choruses.

The King James version of the Scriptures is recommended for memorization as it is the most widely used and best-known version.

Memory Verse Teaching Principles

1. Select short, easy to memorize verses for beginning a memorization program. For some, a few words may be the maximum.

2. Select memory verses that teach specific truths that are appropriate for individual and group needs.

3. Increase the length of the verses or add verses as the students demonstrate the ability to memorize and retain the content.

4. Introduce new verses gradually after the previous verse has been mastered.

5. Explain the meaning of the words as well as the verse.

6. Some verses may be shortened for those who have difficulty in learning.

7. Use visual aids to illustrate the verse including the words and the reference for those who may be able to read.

8. Practice the pronunciation of difficult words.

9. Say the entire verse with the reference before and after the verse.

10. Repeat a word or phrase twice and then have students repeat. Add additional words and phrases.

11. Repeat and review often.

12. Many of the methods of teaching a song may be used in teaching the memory verse.

13. Use a tape recorder for teaching and practice.

14. Use memory verse packets with a new verse added as it is learned.

15. Enlist the help of parents and family members in learning and reviewing memory verses. Suggest that they be incorporated into a family devotional time.

16. Incorporate the verses and their meanings in different parts of a particular program.

17. Use rewards for memorization such as in the AWANA program.

18. Avoid using verses that are similar in content as you begin a memorization program.

19

EXPRESSION OR
ACTIVITY TIME

The **expression time** allows the student to participate in the teaching/ learning process. Since the retarded learn by doing and by repetition, the student is able to use more than one type of input in understanding the Bible lesson. An expression/activity session should be included in every lesson. It may include:

1. Musical participation—rhythm band, walking to see Jesus, choir, etc.

2. Retelling the story—independent recall in their own words, use of pictures, flannelgraph. This will illustrate the three levels of learning, (cognitive, affective, behavioral [See chapter 14]).

3. Demonstrate using all levels of the sensory approach to teaching, such as:

    a. Role playing

    b. Drama

    c. Pantomime

4. Take field trips to a church service, baptismal tank, or other areas in or outside the church.

5. Review games like Tic-Tac-Toe, etc.

6. Handcraft or handwork

Specific ideas may be obtained from a variety of Christian educational publications that are available and may be adapted to meet the needs and capabilities of the retarded. Gearing the handwork to the lesson, yet keeping it on the retardeds' level is, at best, a real challenge. It should be noted that the retarded often have poor eye-hand coordination and poor muscle control. Therefore, they may experience real difficulty in using crayons, scissors or other craft or handwork materials.

Handwork Goals

1. Place the emphasis on pupil participation rather than on teacher completion. Teachers and aides should give help *only* when it is necessary.
2. Emphasize the importance of the process rather than the completion of a perfect product.
3. Provide for growth and practical learning.
4. Provide the opportunity to produce or create.
5. Handwork should not be done in a competitive way.
6. Develop self-expression and self-concept.
7. Provide for the development of perceptual skills (so they may be able to perceive shapes, lines, colors, texture) and motor skills (use of scissors, coloring, painting, drawing).
8. Expose students to experiences in a variety of areas.
9. Develop skills in using and caring for materials and equipment.

Handwork Tips

1. Assess the needs and readiness level of the students so activities may be selected that are within their functional limit.
2. Determine the major curriculum and teaching goals and select things that would guide their expression.
3. Experiment with the project, complete the project, and evaluate the steps in light of the capabilities of your group.
4. Analyze the steps necessary to teach the project to the student and clearly demonstrate each step.
5. Stress the importance of completing one step at a time and doing it well.
6. Plan alternate activities for students who have major difficulties or those who may complete the project early.
7. Projects should be meaningful and useful.
8. Allow for student choice where possible (color, texture, shape, or type).
9. Select projects that may be steps toward the completion of more complex projects.
10. Projects for adults may be designed for completion during leisure time or home study programs.
11. Have all necessary materials and equipment on hand before beginning (provide for adequate storage).
12. Avoid confusion by having only the necessary items available on the table.
13. Avoid the pressure to hurry or be careless.

14. Have adequate aids or helpers available to provide individualized help where necessary.

15. Do not underestimate the retarded students' ability or potential.

16. Be enthusiastic, patient, firm, and reward with praise.

17. Provide protective covering for clothes and rugs where necessary.

18. If a student and teacher are both frustrated with the activity, it is too difficult. Don't be afraid to say, "I'm sorry, but I will help you."

Specific handwork and expression ideas may be found in publications available in community and Christian bookstores and public libraries. In all cases, available ideas need to be assessed and adapted in light of the abilities and needs of the students.

20

LEADING THE RETARDED TO CHRIST

Do the mentally retarded need to be saved? *Can* the retarded be saved? How do you present the gospel to the mentally retarded? These and similar questions inevitably arise when considering any spiritual ministry to the retarded. Such questions are important to parents, family members, pastors and congregations who consider the spiritual needs of the mentally retarded.

From a Biblical and experiential perspective, it is impossible to support such popular conclusions as: 1) the retarded are God's eternal and special children, 2) the retarded never reach the age of accountability and 3) the retarded cannnot be saved because they cannot understand the plan of salvation.

It is not the purpose of this section to present a detailed theological study to settle once and for all the question of accountability; the purpose is to present Biblical principles and practical help in leading the mentally retarded to the Savior. Dogmatic statements about the retarded are not possible because their mental capacities and levels of mental functioning differ drastically. Since they function on a level characteristic of children, the same principles of care and concern that would govern a ministry to children would apply. Those who have worked with the educable (EMR) or trainable (TMR) retarded have found that they are capable of understanding the difference between right and wrong, are capable of understanding basic spiritual truths, and can be saved. The following concepts and principles are presented for your careful consideration:

1. The Bible clearly presents the truth that all have sinned and come short of the glory of God (Rom. 3:23).

2. The Scriptures do not define or address directly the matter of accountability. We can conclude that, in time, people come to a place where they can know and understand what is right or wrong. God requires the individual to act on that basis. We are not to assume or decide conclusively whether a mentally retarded person has or does not have sufficient understanding to be held accountable by God for his sin.

3. Some retarded persons are capable of understanding while others never reach such a level. If they can understand that something is right or wrong, they can understand the gospel.

4. Those whose intellectual capacities never develop beyond the stage of infancy or early childhood will be provided for by the grace of God. (See 2 Samuel 12:23.)

5. We are responsible for clearly presenting the plan of salvation. It is God's responsibility to open the mind and understanding of all people to the truth of the gospel (Ps. 119:130).

6. Because of their mental and learning limitations, the retarded have difficulty understanding symbols and abstract concepts. Biblical truth, therefore, must be presented in concrete, everyday, and practical, real-life themes.

7. The retarded, like small children, want to please and may, therefore, respond to an invitation because of their desire to please, or to gain your attention. Care should be exercised in counseling with the retarded. Find out why they responded and where they are in their knowledge and understanding. Explain carefully and ask questions that require more than a yes or no answer.

8. When presenting the gospel to the mentally retarded, pray for, look for, and expect the Holy Spirit to enable them to understand and respond to the truth. Lead the child to see that what God says in His Word is true. The retarded can and will be saved if we prayerfully and faithfully present the gospel in full dependence upon the Holy Spirit to do His work. Some Biblical truths for thought:

Isaiah 28:10—presents a careful pattern for teaching: "For precept must be upon precept, precept upon precept; line upon line, line upon line; here a little, and there a little."

Psalm 19:7—states the power of the Word of God upon those of limited mental capacity: "The law of the LORD is perfect. converting the soul: the testimony of the LORD is sure, making wise the simple."

1 Corinthians 2:10, 14—outlines the place and work of the Holy Spirit: "But God hath revealed them unto us by His Spirit . . . But the natural man receiveth not the things of the Spirit of God: for they are foolishness unto

him: neither can he know them, because they are spiritually discerned."

The use of the human hand has been an effective means of explaining the gospel to the retarded. Each finger of the hand represents a step in the plan of salvation.

1. I have sinned—Romans 3:23 (thumb)
2. God loves me—John 3:16, Romans 5:8 (index finger)
3. Christ died for me—Romans 5:6, John 3:16 (middle finger)
4. I receive Him—John 1:12, John 3:16 (ring finger)
5. I am saved—Acts 16:31 (little finger)

A detailed consideration of this plan may be found in *Salvation,* a five-lesson series for the mentally retarded avaible from Shepherds, Inc. A single visualized lesson is also available from any Child Evangelism Fellowship Director.

Summary

It is important, in presenting the gospel to and counselling with the retarded, to explain each area carefully. Identify the source as the Word of God. Abundant personal illustrations should be used so that the retarded see the application to themselves. As with all children, care should be exerised to find out where the person is as to his knowledge and understanding. Lead the retarded individual to see what God says in His Word. Remember that the mentally retarded have the same basic spiritual needs as all children and adults. It is also important to realize that all Biblical truth must be presented to the mentally retarded in accordance with their mental age. As their mental age increases, their ability to more easily understand religious or spiritual truth and experience also increases.

21

EFFECTIVE DISCIPLINARY MANAGEMENT

It **was previously** stated that poor behavior is not synonymous with mental retardation. The need to be controlled and governed is universal to all of humanity and is not eliminated by other of life's problems and difficulties. In fact, the desire for boundaries and loving control may be increased. Furthermore, discipline involves much more than punishment for breaking of rules.

There are two basic aspects of discipline presented in the Scripture. In the Old Testament, the word *chasten* is used with the idea of disciplining with blows (punishment) and with words (correction or instruction) or correcting, arguing, disputing, reasoning. The basic word in the New Testament is also translated chasten with the root idea of training up or educating a child by discipline (punishment) and chastening (learning, instructing, teaching). (See Job 5:17; Ps. 94:2; Ps. 118:8; Deut. 21:18; Prov. 3:11; Heb. 12:5–11.)

The following are general guidelines to help in establishing adequate discipline rules and effective teaching and correction.

Establish Reasonable Limits

1. The retarded person must know the boundaries of established rules and principles.

2. Rather closely-set limits are essential since they have difficulty in transferring knowledge from one situation to another.

3. The limits must be within the individual's grasp.

115

4. Reasonable and understood punishment is essential for going beyond the established limits.

5. Teach the students what is right/wrong or acceptable/unacceptable.

6. Give advance warning where possible or practical. Forcing a student to perform too quickly or to stop instantly or to turn abruptly from one activity to another often causes frustration, irritation and conflict.

7. Emphasize the Biblical truth that God holds us accountable for our behavior.

Establish a Stable Routine for Daily Activities

1. Have a set time to eat, play, rest, etc.
2. Deviate as little as possible from the set routine.
3. A busy, occupied, happy person is much easier to control.

Be Certain the Individual Knows What is Expected of Him

1. Do not assume that he knows or remembers just because you told him.
2. He may have to be told and shown many times before he learns.
3. Make sure the individual really understands.
4. Have the individual's attention when you are speaking.
5. Say what you really mean for him to know and understand.
6. Show and practice.

Be Consistent

1. Consistency is a *key* factor in discipline.
2. Do not expect or accept one form of behavior, response or level of achievement today and discipline the same action tomorrow.
3. Do not threaten to do something and fail to carry it out.
4. Decide what the rules/behavior will be and do not deviate.
5. Praise or disapproval should consistently be given for a definite type of behavior.

Be Positive

1. Do not always say "no."
2. If at all possible, introduce some activity that is acceptable to replace that which is undesirable.
3. Think of ways to respond positively even to things for which the ultimate answer is "no."
4. Suggest what the individual should do.
5. Where possible, give the individual a choice of two or more acceptable options.

Make Commands or Requests Short, Simple and Related to the Task

1. Allow time for the individual to think it through and to respond properly.
2. Sometimes they do not obey because adults do not communicate clearly what is expected.
3. Demonstrate where possible.
4. Suggest the next specific task to be performed.

Expect Positive or Good Behavior

Do not emphasize the undesirable behavior. Do not challenge with such statements as, "If you do so and so, I'll. . . ." Let him know what he *should* do rather than what he *should not* do. Reward good behavior.

Do not Give the Individual a Choice Unless You Plan to Abide by His Choice

Make discipline immediate, firm, consistent with the person's mental age, and realistic for the act or offense committed.

Temper Discipline with Love

The retarded are usually anxious to please those whom they love. Love and patience often are the keys to unlocking doors closed by fear and scoldings. However, do not smother the individual with love and lose the ability to communicate firmness and authority.

Sometimes the Retarded Need the Discipline of Experience

1. We have to allow them the privilege of learning the hard way that a hot stove burns the fingers of the one who touches it.
2. Expect reasonable error in judgment when the student experiments in a new area of responsibility.
3. Don't badger, heckle, or overcorrect.
4. Withdraw supervision progressively when the individual is able to assume reasonable responsibility for himself.

Give the Retarded Individual Some Acceptable Outlets for Getting Rid of Hostility, Excess Emotions or Physical Energy

1. You may have to interrupt an activity to exercise or take a walk.

2. An individual may have to go to another room for some one-on-one change of pace activity.

Do Not Discipline When You are Upset/Not in Control

Count slowly to thirty before you respond. If it is impossible, then seek the assistance of someone else.

Be Sure to Pray with the Individual After He Has Calmed Down

Discipline on the Level of the Mental Age of the Child/Adult

Remember the goal is to learn, correct, change, and teach for the glory of the Lord. Rewards and loss of rewards are Biblical truths.

Discipline is Best Done in Private, not in front of an audience.

22

RECREATION, LEISURE TIME, GAMES AND PHYSICAL EDUCATION

In the last decade, the importance of a recreation and leisure time program for the mentally retarded has been realized. Research studies have reported that the retarded spend most of their leisure time at home watching television or listening to the radio (Litton, 1978). Many retarded are isolated in group homes located in areas where there isn't accessibility to recreational programs or facilities. A variety of recreational activities provides opportunity for the development of all areas of a person's life—physical, social, personal—as well as needed active participation. Recreation includes physical education, exercise, leisure time and games. Recreation is also important because the mentally retarded are two to five years behind the national norms in motor performance and ability and, in general, are characterized by poor physical fitness skills (Litton, 1978).

Categories of Involvement

1. Individual Leisure or Play Activity—includes such areas as coloring, magazines, painting, hooked rugs, crafts, electronic games

2. Passive Leisure Activity—areas in which the person is a spectator, including radio, TV, tapes, records, sporting events

3. Game Activity—participation in team or individual games or physical education, including areas such as hiking, bowling, bicycling, exercise programs, swimming, fishing, camping, scouting, softball, basketball, and AWANA

4. Hobby Activities—includes a large variety of areas such as pets, music, collections, crafts, scrap books, and some game areas

5. Socialization Activities—activities or areas that encourage meeting people and developing new friendships. The church programs are very important in development of social skills and graces.

The degree or extent of participation will vary greatly and depend upon the functional level and interests of the retarded who participate. Planning, therefore, must include consideration of these needs and interests. Some of the retarded may be integrated into current church programs such as socials, sports teams, and field trips, while a separate program will need to be scheduled for others. The initial church emphasis may be to include the mentally retarded and their families in existing programs. Programs can then be added to meet specific areas of total need. If you have a Shepherds Sunday School class, socials and trips should be scheduled regularly as part of this program.

Tips for Using Games

Games are effective not only for increasing motivation and learning but also for involvement in recreational-leisure time programming. Some of the mentally retarded can participate in many of the same games and activities as anyone else. Modifications may be necessary in order to be consistent with their interests, needs, abilities, and liabilities.

In planning for games, the general physical limitations of the retarded must be considered. In addition, there probably will be a broad range of physical fitness and ability in any group of retarded. It is advisable to analyze the physical abilities of those who are enrolled. This will help in the planning for and conducting of games and activities. A suggested evaluation sheet is found in Appendix F. The game program will, of necessity, be built around the abilities and needs of those who are attending. In an organized program like AWANA, all enrollees should be evaluated before being placed into the program.

In structuring games:

1. The retarded need to learn to have fun playing and participating in games, to abide by the rules, and to show good sportsmanship.

2. The retarded need to learn to take turns and to work with one or more individuals in friendly participation.

3. Place the emphasis on participation and achievement rather than winning or losing. They need to learn that there are both winners and losers in a game.

4. Switch the emphasis from losing, which identifies with failure, and from winning by beating an opponent, to winning or losing by doing one's best for the Savior.

5. Teach the rules for games and how to play them. Initial games should be simple with as few rules and steps as possible. Advance from the simple to the complex as the participants understand and learn.

6. Give simple, well-explained directions along with a step by step demonstration. Special attention should be given to when and how you begin and stop. Practice informally.

7. If a retarded individual is integrated into a regular game program, place him in the middle of a team and not in a key position.

8. Introduce new skills one at a time. If a skill proves to be too difficult, analyze why and break it down into additional steps where necessary.

9. Use games that stress individual or pairs competition and build this up to the team concept.

10. When dividing into teams, see that the teams are as evenly divided as possible in ability and handicap. Staff should also participate to foster enthusiasm and participation as well as to guide the retarded while running, etc.

11. In using teams, it may be necessary to use simple colored vests with numbers, colored ribbons, etc., to help identify the participants with their team and order of participation.

12. Begin with warm-up type activities to get everyone involved and going.

13. In adapting games or activities, changes may be made in (a) distances and sizes of playing areas, (b) rules, (c) equipment used and (4) skills used or required.

The mentally retarded can make more effective use of their leisure time if proper training and programs are provided. A variety of possibilities are available for involvement by the church in integrated or separate programs.

Appendix A

SAMPLE SUNDAY SCHOOL PROGRAM SCHEDULE

9:30 A.M.	Welcome, taking off coats, etc., greeting one another
9:35 A.M.	Interest Center—provide games and activities—talking with the students allowing them to relate their experiences and things of interest during the last week.
9:45 A.M.	Song Time
9:55 A.M.	Prayer and Praise Time
10:00 A.M.	Announcements, offering
10:05 A.M.	Bible Lesson
10:20 A.M.	Handwork—Expression, Memory Verses, Review
10:30 A.M.	Dismissal

Appendix B

SAMPLE SCHEDULES

Younger Students

1.	Opening Activities	5 minutes
	(Attendance, welcome, remove coats, etc.)	
2.	Prayer	2 minutes
3.	Formal lesson (simple religious concept or Bible story)	10 minutes
4.	Offering	3 minutes
5.	Restroom break	10 minutes
6.	Art activity related to main theme	10 minutes
7.	Exercise time	5 minutes
8.	Singing	5 minutes
9.	Review main points of lesson	5 minutes
10.	Closing	5 minutes

Older Students

1.	Opening Activities	5 minutes
	(Attendance, welcome, remove coats, etc.)	
2.	Prayer (Include discussion of what is meant by words in prayer)	5 minutes
3.	Formal lesson (Doctrinal principle, Bible story etc., using discussion and question techniques)	20 minutes
4.	Offering (emphasizing the purpose)	5 minutes
5.	Acting out the truth of the lesson	15 minutes
6.	Review main points of the lesson	5 minutes
7.	Closing	5 minutes

Source Book

Helping the Retarded to Know God, Hahn & Raasch, pp. 80, 81

Appendix C

THE SHEPHERDS CURRICULUM

The following materials are available for use in developing Sunday School programs for the mentally retarded. All curriculum materials have been thoroughly tested throughout the Shepherds Home with all ages and ability levels.

Format of each series
Information—Teacher Suggestions
Series Overview
Suggested teaching helps (visuals, etc.)
Lessons—
    Aims
    Enrichment Scripture for Teacher
    Memory Verses
    Songs
    Lesson Outline
    Presession Activities
    Lesson
    Activities—Extensive suggestions including patterns
    Review

Please note that each individual lesson is structured to be taught for four weeks. Repetition is *vital*.

1. **Creation**
    6 Lessons: In the Beginning God; God's 3rd Day; God's 4th and 5th Days;

God Made All the Animals; God made Man & Woman; God Rested.
2. **Our Great God**
   8 Lessons: Jesus Helps the Fisherman; Jesus Makes a Home in Heaven for Me; Every Pot Was Filled With Oil; God Cares for a Widow; A Loving Helper—The Good Samaritan; David Helps Mephibosheth; Rebekah, a Good Friend; Jesus Helps Peter Speak the Truth.
3. **We Learn Obedience**
   6 Lessons: Two Men Believe God (Joshua and Caleb); Balaam Disobeys God; Crossing the Jordan River; Gideon Obeys God; Samson Loses His Strength; God's Friend Obeys (Abraham).
4. **We Learn to Worship**
   6 Lessons: We Worship a Holy God; A Place to Worship God; We Worship God on His Day; We Worship God by Singing; God's Word Helps Us to Worship; We Worship God by Praying.
5. **How to Become A Christian**
   (A supplemental series for use at any time)
   5 Short Lessons: All Have Sinned; God Loves Me; Jesus Died for Me; I Receive Jesus; I Am Saved.
6. **Life of David**
   8 Lessons: God's People Want a King; Samuel Warns the People; God Sent Saul to be King; King Saul Disobeyed God; David is Chosen King; David and the Giant; King Saul Dies; David Becomes King.
7. **Miracles of Jesus**
   6 Lessons: Jesus Obeys God's Word; Jesus Turns Water to Wine; Jesus Makes a Sick Boy Well; Jesus Feeds the Five Thousand; Jesus Walks on the Water; Jesus Makes a Blind Man See.
8. **Baptism**
   4 Lessons: Who Should Be Baptized; Why We Should Be Baptized; How We are Baptized (mode); What Does Baptism Mean to Me.
9. **Moses**
   6 Lessons: God Cares for Moses; God Calls Moses; Moses and Pharaoh; God Sends More Plagues; Obey God and Live; Following God's Commands.
10. **Easter—Series I**
    5 Lessons: Jesus and the Last Supper; Jesus Prays in the Garden; Jesus Rides into Jerusalem; Jesus is Crucified; Jesus Lives.
11. **Easter—Series II**
    3 Lessons: Jesus Arrested and Taken Before Pilate; The Price Jesus Paid for Our Sins; Jesus is Alive and is With Us.
12. **Thanksgiving Series**
    A. First Year—2 Lessons: The Man Who Said Thank You; Noah Thanks God for His Care.

B. Second Year—2 Lessons: A Day of Thanks; We Thank God for Jesus.

C. Third Year—2 Lessons: The People Say "Thank You"; The People Say "Thank You" and Obey God.

17. **Special Days**
    A. Valentine's Day—1 Lesson: Showing Love
    B. Patriotic Lesson—1 Lesson: Our Country and Our Flag
    C. Mother's Day—1 Lesson: A Loving Mother
    D. Father's Day—1 Lesson: An Obedient Father

18. **Stories of Paul**
    6 Lessons: Paul as a Boy; Paul and the Church; Paul Becomes a Christian; Paul Escapes to Jerusalem; Paul Becomes a Missionary; Paul in Prison.

19. **Study of the Lord's Prayer**
    10 Lessons: Each phrase of the prayer is a lesson.

20. **People Jesus Knew**
    6 Lessons: John the Baptist; The Disciples; Matthew Follows Jesus; Mary and Martha, Jesus' Friends; The Children; Nicodemus Comes to Jesus.

21. **We Learn About Heaven**
    4 Lessons: Heaven is a Real Place; Who Will Be in Heaven?; What Will Not Be in Heaven?; A Picture of the New Heaven.

22. **Christian Behavior** (Very good for young adults)
    5 Lessons: My Behavior With My Family; My Behavior With Friends; My Behavior at Work; How Do I Handle My Feelings?; My Behavior in Leisure Time.

23. **Saul—Israel's First King**
    6 Lessons: Israel Asks For a King; A King for Israel; An Offering Without God's Blessing; Saul's Hungry Army; The Gift That God Did Not Want; No Longer God's King.

24. **Jonah**
    4 Lessons: The Price of Disobedience; God Gives a Second Chance; A Cry for Repentance; Jonah's Anger Against God.

25. **Abraham's God is Our God**
    6 Lessons: The Call of Abram; Abram and Lot; God Promises Abram a Son; Three Visitors Come to Abraham; Abraham's Test of Faith; Abraham Finds a Bride for Isaac.

26. **Joshua**
    6 Lessons: Joshua Becomes the Leader; Joshua Sends Out Spies; Crossing the Jordan River; The Battle of Jericho; Joshua is Tricked by the Gibeonites; Joshua Teaches the People.

27. **Christian Character and Conduct**
    6 Lessons: Obedience—Three Men in a Fiery Furnace; Thoughtfulness—Dorcas Thinks of Others; Forgiveness—A Servant Who Would Not Forgive His Friend; Unselfishness—The Man Who Wanted Everything for Himself; Thankfulness—One Man Says "Thank You"; Truthfulness—The Servant Who Lied.
28. **Christian Character and Conduct #2**
    5 Lessons: Compassion—The Good Samaritan; Contentment—God's People Grumble; Faithfulness—Troubles Didn't Stop Paul; Courage—Daniel in the Lions' Den; Humility—Who is the Greatest?
29. **23rd Psalm**

A DVBS curriculum is also available.

Other titles will be advertised in our bi-monthly newsletter, *The Shepherds Folder,* as they are available. Each series is available for a $2.00 donation.

Order items by title from: Shepherds Home and School
                        Box 400
                        Union Grove, WI 53182

Appendix D

PREPLACEMENT EVALUATION

Name: _____ Date: _____

Tester: _____

(An asterisk indicates further comments at the end of the evaluation)

I. **Attention Span**

_____ Short   _____ Average   _____ Below Average

Frustration indicated by:

II. **Personal Data**	YES	NO
Student knows:		
A. His name	_____	_____
B. His age	_____	_____
C. His address	_____	_____
D. His telephone number	_____	_____
E. How many brothers and sisters	_____	_____
F. His brothers' and/or sisters' names	_____	_____
G. His birthdate	_____	_____

III. **Colors**		
A. Can identify colors in a group (ex. pick out the red or blue)	_____	_____
B. Can match colors but doesn't know the name	_____	_____
C. Can identify colors verbally	_____	_____

IV. **Gross Motor Coordination**
   A. Can catch a ball   _____   _____
   B. Can kick a ball   _____   _____
   C. Can kick a moving ball   _____   _____
   D. Can throw a ball in the wastebasket   _____   _____
   E. Uses left hand and foot   _____   _____
   F. Uses right hand and foot to
      accomplish the tasks   _____   _____

V. **Fine Motor Coordination**
   A. Can color a picture   _____   _____
   B. Stays in the lines   _____   _____
   C. Scribbles   _____   _____
   D. Made no attempt   _____   _____
   E. Can hold a pencil   _____   _____
   F. Peg board pattern   _____   _____
   G. Lacing   _____   _____
   H. Puzzles
      1. simple, one piece   _____   _____
      2. five piece puzzles   _____   _____
      3. ten piece puzzles   _____   _____

VI. **Time Concepts**
   Knows terms for:
   A. Morning   _____   _____
   B. Night   _____   _____
   C. Today   _____   _____
   D. Tomorrow   _____   _____
   E. Yesterday   _____   _____
   F. A week   _____   _____
   G. A month   _____   _____
   H. Days of the week   _____   _____
   I. Can say the months   _____   _____
   J. Can tell time by the hour   _____   _____
   K. Can tell time by the half-hour   _____   _____
   L. Can tell time by fifteen minutes   _____   _____
   M. Can tell time by five minutes   _____   _____

VII. **Shapes and Designs**
   A. Identification
      1. Circle   _____   _____
      2. Square   _____   _____

    3. Triangle   _____   _____

    4. Diamond   _____   _____

    5. Rectangle   _____   _____

  B. Can produce with pattern

    1. Circle   _____   _____

    2. Square   _____   _____

    3. Triangle   _____   _____

    4. Diamond   _____   _____

    5. Rectangle   _____   _____

    6. Verticle line   _____   _____

    7. Horizontal line   _____   _____

  C. Can produce without pattern

    1. Circle   _____   _____

    2. Square   _____   _____

    3. Triangle   _____   _____

    4. Diamond   _____   _____

    5. Rectangle   _____   _____

  D. Can follow simple designs

    1. Peg board patterns   _____   _____

    2. Parquetry blocks   _____   _____

      Comments:

VIII. **Can Write His Name**

  A. First name   _____   _____

  B. Reverses letters   _____   _____

  C. Last name   _____   _____

  D. Reverses letters   _____   _____

IX. **Money**

  A. Matches coins   _____   _____

    1. Penny   _____   _____

    2. Nickel   _____   _____

    3. Dime   _____   _____

    4. Quarter   _____   _____

    5. Dollar   _____   _____

  B. Identification

    1. Penny   _____   _____

    2. Nickel   _____   _____

    3. Dime   _____   _____

    4. Quarter   _____   _____

    5. Dollar   _____   _____

C. Can tell how much money in a:
1. Penny
2. Nickel _____ How many pennies
3. Dime _____ How many pennies _____Nickels
4. Quarter _____ How many pennies _____ Nickels _____How many nickels and dimes
D. Can count out money
1. Count out 35¢   _____   _____
2. Count out 65¢   _____   _____
3. Count out 15¢   _____   _____
4. Count out 10¢   _____   _____

X. **Numbers**
A. Rote count to 25   _____   _____
B. Can match numbers to 25   _____   _____
1, 2, 3, 4, 5, 6, 7, 8, 9, 10   _____   _____
11, 12, 13, 14, 15, 16, 17, 18, 19, 20 _____   _____
21, 22, 23, 24, 25   _____   _____
C. Can write numbers in sequence to 25
1, 2, 3, 4, 5, 6, 7, 8, 9, etc   _____   _____
D. Can identify numbers out of sequence
to 25   _____   _____
E. Can do simple number problems (sets) _____   _____
F. Can count by 5s to 100   _____   _____
G. Can count by 10s to 100   _____   _____

XI. **Communication**
A. Uses gestures   _____   _____
B. Uses phrases   _____   _____
C. Uses sentences   _____   _____

    Comments:

D. Knows the meanings of these words—
can follow directions
1. Up   _____   _____
2. Down   _____   _____
3. Top   _____   _____
4. Bottom   _____   _____
5. On   _____   _____
6. Off   _____   _____
7. Pull   _____   _____
8. Push   _____   _____

9. Front	———	———
10. Back	———	———
E. Can follow:		
1. Simple one step direction	———	———
2. More than two step direction	———	———
3. A series of directions	———	———

XII. **Personal Needs**

A. Buttons	———	———
B. Zips	———	———
C. Laces	———	———
D. Ties (shoes, hat, etc.)	———	———
E. Can put on:		
1. Hat	———	———
2. Coat	———	———
3. Boots	———	———

Additional Comments:

Appendix E

GAME EVALUATION GUIDE

The following are suggested areas of evaluation to be used by the game director in selecting the games and physical activities for the group. The guide surveys the children's physical capabilities or limitations, game understanding and sense of game participation.

1. **Walking**—Able to walk slowly while following a straight line on the floor? Able to walk faster while following a straight line on the foor?
2. **Running**—Able to run the length of room and back? Able to run one lap around the gym? How does he run?
3. **Crawling**—Able to crawl a prescribed distance on hands and knees? Able to crawl around obstacles without tipping them over?
4. **Sit-ups**—Number of sit-ups done by the clubber.
5. **Skipping**—Able to skip the length of room?
6. **Jumping**—Able to stand still and jump over an obstacle? Able to jump rope? Able to jump off an object and maintain balance?
7. **Hopping**—Able to lift left foot, balance, and hop on the right foot? Reverse?
8. **Throwing**—Able to throw a ball, football, bean bag, to another person overhand? Underhand? Able to throw ball or bean bag into a waste basket at distance of 8′ to 10′?
9. **Balance**—Note performance in hopping or skipping tasks.
10. **Following Directions**—In Simon Says drill? Simple games?
11. **Directionality**—Up, down, right, left, forward, backward
12. **Catching**—A tennis ball—short distance? Long Distance?
    A soft ball—short distance? Long distance?
    A bean bag—short distance? Long distance?
    A volley ball—short distance? Long distance?
13. Able to bounce a ball while standing still? While running?
14. Able to run and pass a baton to someone else?

Appendix F

INDIVIDUAL PRESCRIPTIVE TEACHING PLAN

Name: _____ Birthdate: _____ Area of Placement: _____

Date: _____ Staff Responsible for Implementation of Program: _____

Areas of Concern	Goals to be Accomplished	Methods of Accomplishing Goals: Tasks, services, activities used to reach goal	Attainment

I Spiritual _____

II Social/
Emotional Maturity _____

III Vocational
Skills _____

IV Academics _____

V Physical
Education _____

VI Speech
Therapy _____

VII Motor Skills
(gross/fine) _____

VIII Self-help
    Skills   _____

 IX Leisure Time
    Activities   _____

  X Other _____

Profile Report   _____

Goals Accomplished from last report:

Spiritual:
Social/Emotional:
Vocational:
Academics:
Physical Education:
Speech Therapy:
Motor Skills:
Self-help Skills:
Leisure Time:

_____

_____

_____

_____

_____

_____

_____

_____

_____

_____

_____

Appendix G

THE STORY OF SHEPHERDS MINISTRY

And I will set up Shepherds over them . . . (Jer. 23:4)

The Stewards Sunday School Class of the Garfield Baptist Church of Milwaukee was composed of young married couples—just ordinary people doing ordinary jobs. They were busy raising their families and struggling with the problems common to all of us in this complex world. But God had a job for His ordinary children to do.

One winter evening in 1957, this class met for a social time. A short business meeting was held and a time of "brainstorming" developed. The class had talent and ambition; its members were anxious to channel some of their energy. One after another, ideas and suggestions were tossed out for discussion. In the midst of all the clatter, quiet, soft-spoken Lawrence Cayton asked to say a word.

"Could the class possibly do something to help retarded children?"

Mr. Cayton's second child was a Down's Syndrome. For several years, he and his wife had been trying to find a satisfactory permanent home for nine-year-old Larry. They were made sadly aware of the fact that most of the state and privately owned institutions are hopelessly overcrowded or too expensive. Would the Stewards Class be interested in investigating this problem?

One of the teachers of the class, Dr. Viggo B. Olsen, now a medical missionary in Bangladesh, organized a committe of eleven couples to look into this situation; Dr. and Mrs. Glenn Franke were asked to be co-chairmen. None realized to what they were committing themselves.

They called themselves the Committee on Mental Retardation and held

137

their first meeting on February 7, 1957. Nine people attended. It was here that they caught a glimpse of what the future held. In an awkward fashion, they took their first steps.

A short portion of the minutes of this meeting reads as follows: "The most insurmountable obstacles seemed to dwindle away as the discussion progressed and the early plans were made. It was precious joy to behold the sincere interest in the heart of each committee member. God has promised in Psalm 37:5, 'Commit thy way unto the Lord; trust also in Him; and He shall bring it to pass.' We have placed our plans at His feet and will proceed with the assurance that He will guide."

This was the feeling of those who met that first night and the consistent force throughout hundreds of meetings that have followed.

Believing without question that all things should be done "decently and in order," the class launched their program. They presented it to their pastor, Dr. William E. Kuhnle, and the board of deacons. They moved on to the Council of Fourteen of the General Association of Regular Baptist Churches. Their first meeting with the Council took place December 10, 1957, in Chicago. They wanted the Council's approval to circularize our Association with literature and personnel.

The committee assured the Council that one of their goals was to show the world that Christians do care about the practical needs of their fellow men. They even read excerpts of letters they had received from parents of retarded children. When they finished their presentation, two or three of the Council members were wiping tears from their eyes. It was about then that Dr. Robert T. Ketcham siad in a most matter-of-fact tone, "Well, now, how much is all this going to cost—$250,000?" The Council didn't give any money that day—or since—but their encouragement was all that was needed.

A Sunday School class was soon organized at Garfield for retarded children and a day-care program was set up for Larry Cayton, assuring his mother of one day a week to call her own. Letters were sent to all the Regular Baptist churches; a list of retarded children in the GARBC churches was compiled. There was certainly a need for this project, but shouldn't they stop there? In some measure, the needs of the Cayton family were being met. Wasn't that one of the primary goals the Stewards Class wanted to accomplish?

Maybe it was all those heart-rending letters from mothers and fathers of retarded children. Maybe it was the fact that many of us live out our lifetimes and leave nothing for generations that follow. Maybe it was because they were in so deep they couldn't stop the wheels of activity. And maybe—and there really is no maybe here—it was because Shepherds was ordained by God to do something in a positive, practical fashion for mentally retarded children.

The little committee changed! Some tried and true workers moved on to other fields of service and several new faces joined the group.

It was during the second summer that they chose the name "Shepherds." This name was selected from an Old Testament verse (Jer. 23:4) and seemed so ideally suited for this endeavor that when they incorporated on July 31, 1958, this was the name used.

They presented Shepherds through every possible means. They traveled to Columbus, Ohio in 1958 and with handmade materials even had the courage to set up a display at the annual conference of the GARBC. They made many speeches. They wrote letters by the hundreds and mimeographed and mailed thousands more. They also wrote tracts and a little booklet, and much to their amazement saw these gain nationwide recognition for Shepherds. They started a bi-monthly newsletter and held their first Shepherds Sunday on November 13, 1960. After several abortive attempts, they drew up a constitution and elected a board of directors.

The board sensed that if the ministry were to reach its goal, they would need to search out a man to direct the work. In 1961, Dr. Andrew H. Wood was called to be the executive director, a task he assumed August 1 of that year.

By 1963, property had been pruchased in Union Grove (25 miles south of Milwaukee), building plans drawn and approved, financing arranged and construction of Unit 1 begun. The doors to this Christ-centered haven opened on June 6, 1964, to admit the first 36 boys and girls.

Building programs in 1966, 1969, 1971 and 1974 have seen expansion of the Home to six buildings currently providing for 130 residents. The work has expanded to require a staff of 79.

God has led this unique ministry from a plaintive cry in 1957, to a 130 bed home and school valued at $3.1 million in 1983. Indeed, Shepherds stands as a living testimony to an exceedingly, abundantly able God. Countless thousands have been touched by this ministry.

A resident family of 130 children and adults, plus local day students, is no small challenge for the dedicated staff at Shepherds. Chronologically, these students range from 10 to 60 years of age. Their mental age span ranges from 6 months to 15 years. The facility administration, modular administrators, along with numerous other staff members, spend considerable time determining the proper program for each student. Changes are made as they are needed, thus a student always moves along at his own rate of progress.

Students up to 18 years of age attend the on-campus boarding school September through June. Here they are grouped according to age, size, intellect, social level and coordination development. The instructional level of each class is determined by curriculum designed to meet individual as well as group needs. Bible, basic skills in communication, self-care, personal hygiene, coordination activities, physical education, recreation and academic subjects comprise their program. The overall goal for the school is to prepare each student for living in the world which may eventually be their own home, the community or even Shepherds.

All adults are involved in one of several specialized living and working modules year round. The adult activity center provides a structured program with emphasis on minimal work and social skills for the profoundly retarded. The craft center meets the needs of those who can produce craft items that are in turn sold to the public. The level I work activity center offers a highly supervised workshop. The level II work activity center provides a setting for those who can achieve a variety of job skills and work under limited supervision. The community living skills area prepares select adults for living more independently. Adult academics are part of this program. A sheltered employee program selecting residents from the various adult programs, provides jobs for the more capable adults. Here they find meaningful employment in the kitchen, laundry, housekeeping and maintenance departments of Shepherds. Community employment is provided for selected adults as jobs are available. These programs offer a wide range of activities thus encompassing the abilities of all adults living at Shepherds.

Running throughout the entire program of Shepherds is an outstanding spiritual training emphasis. Sunday School, church, midweek prayer meeting, a weekly chapel service, daily morning and evening devotions plus daily Bible classes round out this unique aspect of the work. Rich fruit results from the untiring efforts of the staff. Continuity is provided as all spiritual training is based upon a prescribed curriculum. This Bible curriculum is now available for use in local churches working with the mentally retarded.

Beyond the ministry in Union Grove, the influence of Shepherds permeates churches from coast to coast. Many are organizing and conducting Shepherds' Sunday School classes, worship services, weekly Bible studies, AWANA and youth programs, Christian day school classes, etc., thus reaching the mentally retarded and their families through the local church.

In 1979, Shepherds College of Special Education was established. During the academic year, Shepherds' staff teach at several fundamental Christian colleges. This program is designed to train young people in a Christian philosophy of Special Ed and prepare them for ministries in Christian day schools and the local church. Summer school classes are taught at Shepherds Home and School in Union Grove from May through August. The Home also provides the setting for practicums and internships. Several fundamental Christian colleges use the summer program to provide a major or minor in special education for their students.

Inquiries concerning Shepherds' ministries should be made to: Shepherds, Inc., Box 400, Union Grove, WI 53182 1597

* BIBLIOGRAPHY AND RESOURCES

Books from a Religious Perspective

Bogardus, La Donna, ed. *Camping with Retarded Persons.* Nashville: United Methodist Church, 1970.

Christian Education for the Mentally Retarded in Local Congregations. Information Bulletin 82277, St. Louis: Board of Parish Education, The Lutheran Church—Missouri Synod.

Clark, Dahl, Conzenbach. *Look At Me, Please Look At Me.* Elgin, IL: David C. Cook, 1973, 128 pp.

_____ . *Teach Me, Please Teach Me.* Elgin, IL: David C. Cook, 1974, 142 pp.

Cornwall, Thomas and Judson. *Please Accept Me.* Plainfield, NJ: Logos International, 1979, 128 pp.

Hahn, Hans and Werner H. Raasch. *Helping the Retarded to Know God.* St Louis: Concordia Pub. House, 1969, 112 pp.

Hawley, Gloria H. *How to Teach the Mentally Retarded.* Wheaton, IL: Victor Books, 1979, 48 pp.

Hooten, Jean C. *Happy Time Course, 52 Lessons for the Mentally Retarded.* Wheaton IL, 1977.

Lightner, Robert P. *Heaven for Those Who Can't Believe.* Des Plaines, IL: Regular Baptist Press, 1978.

Monroe, Doris D. *Reaching and Teaching Mentally Retarded Persons.* Nashville, Convention Press, 1980, 144 pp.

Perske, Robert. *New Directions for Parents of Persons Who Are Retarded.* Nashville: Abingdon, 1973.

Pierson, James O. *77 Dynamic Ideas for the Christian Education of the Handicapped.* Cincinnati: Standard Pub. 1977, 48 pp.

Roberts, Nancy. *Helps for Parents of a Handicapped Child.* St. Louis: Concordia Publishing House, 1981, 48 pp.

————— . *You and Your Retarded Child*. St. Louis: Concordia Publishing House, 1974, 77 pp.
Stubblefield, Harold W. *The Church's Ministry in Mental Retardation*. Nashville: Broadman Press, 1960, 1965.
Towns, Elmer and Roberta L. Groff. *Successful Ministry to the Retarded*. Chicago: Moody Press, 1972, 144 pp.
Welborn, Terry and Stanley Williams. *Leading the Mentally Retarded in Worship*. St. Louis: Concordia Publishing House, 1973, 31 pp.
Wilke, Harold. *Creating the Caring Congregation*. Nashville: Abingdon, 1980, 110 pp.

Personal Interest Reading

Baptista, Bob and Martha. *Ric*. Chicago: Moody Press, 1981.
Carpenter, Robert. *Why Can't I Learn?* Glendale, CA: Gospel Light Publications, 1972.
Cobb, Mary Ann. *Lorie, A Story of Hope*. New York: Thomas Nelson Publishers, 1979.
Dougan, Isbell and Vyas. *We Have Been There*. Nashville: Abingdon Press, 1983.
Finnie, Nancy R. *Handling the Young Cerebral Palsied Child at Home*. New York: E. P. Dutton Co.
Haggai, John Edmund. *My Son Johnny*. Wheaton, IL: Tyndale House, 1978.
Hawley, Gloria Hope. *Laura's Psalm*. Rolling Meadows, IL: Action House, Inc., 1977.
————— . *Laura's Legacy*. Nashville, TN: Impact Books, 1982.
Krentel, Mildred. *Melissa Comes Home*. New York: Popular Library, 1972.
Monty, Shirlee. *May's Boy*. Nashville: Thomas Nelson Publishers, 1981.
Schultz, Edna M. *They Said Kathy Was Retarded*. Chicago: Moody Press, 1963.
Vanderford, Jennifer R. *Joy Cometh in the Morning*. Eugene, OR: Harvest House Publishers, 1982.
Wheeler, Bonnie. *Challenged Parenting*. Ventura, CA: Regal Books, 1983.
Worswick, Marilyn E. *Thank You Davey, Thank You God*. Minneapolis: Augsburg, 1978.

Articles

Colvin, Elaine Wright. "Handling the Disabled Among Us." *Moody Monthly* (October 1982): 14, 15.
Cornell, George W. "Rules on Retarded Stir Church Uproar." *Racine Journal Times* (Racine, Wisconsin) (May 31, 1980).
Eareckson, Joni. "If God's Not Embarrassed, Why Are We?" *Moody Monthly* (October 1982): 18–20.
Glanville, E. Ellen. "The Whole Church for the Whole Family." *Baptist Bulletin* (December 1969) 11, 12, 23.
Howell, Dorthea. "When the Church Mainstreams." *Moody Monthly* (February 1983): 64-66
Huff, Olson. "Now Smart Enough for Church." *Christianity Today* (August 7, 1981): 24-26.

Krentel, David P. "A Survey of Ministry to the Retarded." Unpublished Doctor of Ministry paper, Dallas Theological Seminary, 1980.

Wheeler, Bonnie. "It Takes Only One or Two Caring People to Start a Caring Church." *Moody Monthly* (October 1982): 16, 17.

Textbooks

Chinn, Drew and Logan. *Mental Retardation A Life Cycle Approach.* 2nd Ed. St. Louis: C. V. Mosby, 1979.

Dobson, James C. and Richard Koch. *The Mentally Retarded Child and His Family, a Multidisciplinary Handbook.* New York: Brunner-Mazel Publishing, 1976.

Grossman, Herbert J., ed. *Classification in Mental Retardation.* Washington, DC: American Association on Mental Deficiency, 1983.

Litton, Freddie W. *Education of the Trainable Mentally Retarded.* St. Louis: C. V. Mosby Co., 1978.

Payne, James S. and James R. Patton. *Mental Retardation.* Columbus, OH: Charles E. Merrill Publishing Co., 1981.

Robinson and Robinson. *The Mentally Retarded Child.* 2nd ed. St. Louis: McGraw Hill Pub. Co., 1976.

Resources

Oosterveen and Cook. *Serving the Mentally Impaired, A Resource Guide for Pastors and Church Workers.* Elgin, IL: David C. Cook, 1983, 52 pp.

National Association for Retarded Children
2709 Avenue E. East
Arlington, TX 76010
(General and Religious Bibliography and list of publications)
(Address of nearest local chapter)

Superintendent of Documents
U.S. Printing Office
Washington, DC
(Bibliography of available publications on mental retardation)

State Department of Education
Special Education Department
(Your State)
(Curriculum Guide for Mental Retardation and list of publications)

*Note: Listing in this section does not necessarily indicate Shepherds' approval of content.